PRAISE FO

YOUR LION INSIDE

"*Your Lion Inside* **is a masterpiece.** Drawing on her years of professional and personal experience, Kim effortlessly weaves together conversation and stories with practical explanations and exercises to help readers activate their greatest potential. She expertly identifies blocks that can keep all of us from living large and offers step-by-step solutions for overcoming them. This book is a comprehensive resource balanced beautifully with depth and heart. Kim's use of the Sisterhood is nothing short of brilliant to illustrate relatable examples to which her readers can really connect. I highly recommend this book. It has quickly become one of my most frequent go-to's on my bookshelf."

—Tara L. Robinson
Hay House author of *The Ultimate Risk* and radio show host

"*Your Lion Inside* **is one of the most important books for our time**, providing new tools and stories to endow women with the power, strength, and hope necessary to allow them to shift into new ways of thinking and to live confident lives, where they are using all of their potential for the greater good of everyone. In a world which is still extremely challenging for women from any background or country, *Your Lion Inside* is one of the most clearly written and highly engaging guides for female empowerment and actualization. Kimberly Faith has created an accessible yet deeply profound method for helping women understand the unseen narratives that are holding them back."

—Maria Moraes Robinson
Coauthor of *Holonomics: Business Where People and Planet Matter* and *Customer Experiences with Soul*, BRAZIL

"My dear Kim, Your wonderful work continues to amaze and comfort me. 'Amaze' because the insight you share with your readers is so full of wisdom that I feel you've lived at least two very full lives! 'Comforted' because knowing that people all over the world will read your work gives me hope for future of humanity. Thank you for inspiring me to live the best life I can possibly live... and for showing the way for so many others to improve the world around them by improving their own lives."

—Bill Timoney
Professional Acting Coach to Bryan Cranston, star of AMC series *Breaking Bad* & Broadway Actor in NETWORK

"This is not a book that tells us 'how' we should be as women, this is a book that will help us understand and consciously choose the impact we have for our future world.

Kim's passion for helping women nurture the very best and most powerful version of themselves, and in turn, pass this insight onto others is a thread running throughout *Your Lion Inside*, interspersed with equal parts humour, humility, and fierceness.

Having worked directly with Kim, I love the fact that the essence of Kim and her life are woven into the book as though it were a tapestry she had sown. You can't read the book without taking away something of Kim and her joie de vivre."

—R. Greedy
Vice President, multinational corporation,
UNITED KINGDOM

"*The glass ceiling is also a mirror* is a powerful statement. Kim masterfully translates how this uniquely manifests itself in each of us through beautifully told 'real-life' stories. She brilliantly uses their unique voices to make it relatable to all of us. There has never been a better time to break the cycle!"

—Angie Hemmelgarn
CHRO, Chief Human Resources Officer,
Global Business Executive

"*Your Lion Inside* is a great read—with a fresh perspective to consciously shift beyond our inherent DNA. The affirmations and scenarios are powerful tools to pause, reflect, and choose. This book is a highly valuable resource for women across the globe who want to be daring and create a new narrative."

—Kiran Jawahrani
Senior Director, multinational corporation, INDIA

"This book is a real story that we face every day—the story is universal. We have learned not to trust in who we are. Kim's book helped me accept my power of presence and my own lion inside. I want other women to have the same experience of freedom."

—Dr. Jade Taihee Chung
re:BOX Consulting Chief Executive Officer, KOREA/ASIA

"I encourage everyone, not only females, to read this inspiring book: Females must read as they will find something from their lives in the stories of the Sisterhood of Seven and as they will reflect to find their lion inside. Males must read to better understand how they can collaborate to make the world a better place for their sisters, wives, and daughters.

Awareness is the first step in seeing the world differently. And Kim's book helps readers to awaken."

—Sibel Bostanci
Executive, Region Learning & Development,
(Middle East-Africa-Turkey-South Asia), TURKEY

"If self-empowerment is the pathway out of the women's victim mentality trap—and it is—then this book provides the roadmap. Through shining a light on the biases and inner dialogue that hold women back from realizing our full potential, Kim Faith unleashes the lion inside our societally acceptable kittenish demeanor. To read the stories of the seven personified mental models is to tease out our own innermost beliefs about our capabilities as women and thus realign ourselves with our worth as workplace and society contributors. Fellow sisters, let's hear you roar!"

—Lori Ehrman Tinkey
Assistant Director, Research & Analysis, ACADEMIA

"Kim's book helped me END THE EXCUSES. I realized the opportunity I had been waiting for was looking in the mirror. Regardless of circumstances or injustices, I now know I have power. And the beautiful part of *Your Lion Inside* is the inspiration to not only use that power for myself, but in the lifting up of my sisters. 'There's enough for me and you.'"

—Angela Russel
Innovative content producer, Award-winning storyteller, Co-Host, Take 5, SEATTLE

"The book was like looking in a mirror....I could relate, first hand, to so many of the stories and anecdotes in the book. I have been so fortunate in my career to have role models and mentors who have pulled me along.

It reinforced the need to double down and do even more for other women who are further behind me in their careers. The advice, suggestions and push to try things make this book unique in its approach. I would recommend it for any women at any point in her career as it serves as a good reminder that we all have the potential to live out our dreams but that we all need help along the way"

—S.D.
Private Equity/Finance, NEW YORK CITY

"Kim Faith has written a highly engaging and provocative book that leads the reader through the journey of the seven most compelling women who live their self-narrative. Narratives which many women encounter at some point in their life.

This book is timely. Having entered into the world of global relationships, women have now found themselves in need of deeper, more trusting, and better developed relationships, at all levels within their organizations, and with themselves. Women are at the height of building their businesses, their presence, and their future from the strength of those relationships.

Second, this book is relevant. I believe that women are seeking to find how to remove the potential barriers, which can often times be themselves, in order to reach not only success, but sustainable success and satisfaction. We find ourselves in a constant struggle of defining and understanding our relationship to the many factors that constitute the founding of a fulfilling life.

Finally, this book is actionable. Women today need to see themselves as the bedrock of the future. They need to keep their minds engaged but not at the expense of their hearts. That is what successful women know and practice. That is one of the things that *Your Lion Inside* does so well—Kim gives us practical, specific actions we can take to avoid the traps and 'time-wastes' of getting in our own way.

Kim has great knowledge and understanding of the female brain and mindset. What makes sense, how it can get off track, and the never-ending cycle of 'Am I good enough?' She has successfully shed light on the endless confusion surrounding the role of women and the healing that needs to take place to show up at our best in everything we do and who we bring to the table."

—Karen Keller Ph.D.
Founder & CEO, Keller Institute™

"To quote Paul Harvey, 'And now the rest of the story...' Your book sat in my stack of self-help books for some time. When packing for a weekend of camping with my kids, I threw it in my bag along with a couple others. Well, once I started reading, I couldn't consume it fast enough. . .

It changed me and my thinking. I suddenly realized I was holding the power all along, the power to look within myself, reflect on my thoughts and actions, and harness that power to show up in my life differently. It's a process, but I am on the path and charging forward.

You sharing your story and journey was a key game changer as I finalized my divorce, bought my own house for me and my three kids, continue to financially support all of us. I was even brave enough to take some chances at work which led me in some directions I never would have thought possible.

I wanted to encourage you to keep going—you are changing lives and I couldn't be more grateful to you. Thank you sister!"

—**J.C.**
Tech Industry

your LION INSIDE

Discover the Power Within
& Live Your Fullest Life

KIMBERLY FAITH

Systems Thinking Expert & Futurist

Advantage.

*Is it possible that hope for humanity is trapped
in the hearts of women?*

Published by Advantage, Charleston, South Carolina.
Member of Advantage Media Group.

ADVANTAGE is a registered trademark, and the Advantage colophon is a trademark of Advantage Media Group, Inc.

Printed in the United States of America.

10 9 8 7 6 5 4 3 2 1

Publisher's Cataloging-In-Publication Data
(Prepared by The Donohue Group, Inc.)

Names: Faith, Kimberly, author.
Title: Your lion inside : discover the power within & live your fullest
    life / Kimberly Faith.
Description: Charleston, South Carolina : Advantage®, [2019] | Previously
    published as: Your lion inside : tapping into the power within. [United
    States] : KF Enterprises, ©2017. | Includes bibliographical references.
Identifiers: ISBN 9781642251159
Subjects: LCSH: Women executives--Psychology. | Leadership in women. |
    Self-actualization (Psychology) in women. | Self-perception in women. |
    Feminism--United States--History.
Classification: LCC HD6054.3 .F35 2019 | DDC 658.409082--dc23

ISBN: 978-1-64225-115-9
LCCN: 2019915684

Cover design by Jamie Earley.
Layout design by Wesley Strickland.

This publication is designed to provide accurate and authoritative information in regard to the subject matter covered. It is sold with the understanding that the publisher is not engaged in rendering legal, accounting, or other professional services. If legal advice or other expert assistance is required, the services of a competent professional person should be sought.

Dedicated to my #sweetsisters around the globe—
past, present, and future.

CONTENTS

A GIFT FOR YOU

The reality is that we have an enemy far greater than any regime, any organizational intent, any unconscious bias, any principle designed to keep us in our place. There are times when we battle the collective because the culture is overpowering—distorting the view for all.

In many places around the world, the battle for the rights of women is still going on—as it should. But while we are looking at that foe, another is trying to sneak in.

Slowly. In stealth mode. Insidious. Quiet, yet so pervasive many don't see it.

Blinded to reality much like a fish is to water.

I saw it and want you to see it too.

As long as we believe the answer is out there—above us, below us, beside us—we will never fully embrace the real source of our power. Each morning when you look in the mirror, in your reflection is the answer you seek.

This manifesto of hope serves as a light in the darkness. A manual of truth. A balm for the battered soul who knows, deep down, there is so much more. Driven by a deep-seated desire to be more, do more, give more.

Therein lies the paradox.

You are already enough. More than enough.

Together, let us remove the dust that has dimmed the treasure. Let us gently begin polishing what is underneath— for you and the whole world to see.

I am enough, and so are you,

Kim

Awareness is the first step in seeing the world differently.

*When we are in "it," it's like swimming in a
fishbowl. Awareness plucks you out of the fishbowl,
shakes you off, and sets you down next to it,
allowing you to see clearly for the first time.*

When your perspective changes, everything begins to shift.

*Is it possible that your conscious mind has been telling you
one story, but your unconscious mind has been writing a
different one?*

The time has come to disrupt yourself.

BREAKING FREE

"We can't take a bag of change here, lady!" the clerk said gruffly and loudly. The seven people behind me in line waiting to check out all stared at me. *All I want to do is buy three gallons of gas so I can see my daughter,* I wanted to scream. Instead, I turned and ran out of the store, clutching my bag of change with tears streaming down my face. It was June 2008, and the price of gas had skyrocketed to over four dollars a gallon.[1] I dumped the change onto the seat of my car, pulled out the quarters, and went back in to purchase one gallon of gas. I wanted to see my daughter before she left for school.

In our few precious minutes together, my daughter's happiness filled me with the fuel I needed to last another day. After saying goodbye, I drove to the storage building where everything I owned was stuffed into a ten-by-ten unit. While searching for a change of clothes, I stumbled and fell. Rage, blame, and fear claimed what little sanity I had left. I remember sitting on the floor, my back up against the wall, looking out at the clear blue sky and asking myself, "How did I get here?"

The day progressively got worse—calls from one debt collector after another, voice mails with threats from an investor relationship gone terribly wrong. I was separated from the husband at the time, and we were alternating months as to who would live in the house with our daughter, Heather. It was my turn to live away, but I had nowhere to go. I had no money in my checking account, no credit card that worked, and the start-up I had so passionately launched was crashing around me. All I had was that damn bag of change.

I remember vividly coming to terms with the fact that things were so messed up the world would be better without me. I was driving down Interstate 85 alongside a section of cement medians, and it hit me that with a simple flick of a wrist, it could be over. The pain could end. The temptation was *so strong*. Just think of all the problems it would solve. The million-dollar life insurance policy would take care of everyone. I would not be able to make any more wrong decisions. Everyone would heal and move on. I was a failure. What value could I possibly have left?

Emotionally, I crossed a dangerous line that night. In the darkness and tears, I had a flashback to something I used to teach in systems thinking. *Structures drive behavior,*[2] I would tell audiences. Right then, I made a rule—a structure—that I would not ride on the highway again at night. And I didn't for nine months while I fought to save Sassytails, the company my daughter and I started.

I don't know when it happened. I don't know *how* it happened. But somewhere along the way, I decided I didn't want my story to end that way. I made a conscious choice to teach my daughter *how to fail with grace.*[3]

That dark time in my life forced me to reevaluate everything I once knew and believed.

TIME IS AN ILLUSION

The afternoon of Wednesday, March 7, 2017, began in a remarkably mundane manner. On the way home, I stopped to vacuum my car. When I inserted my first quarter into the slot, it wouldn't fit. *Broken again?* I thought. But no, my quarters were too big. How did that happen? I looked closer—in my hand were several Susan B. Anthony coins. *Haven't seen those in a while.* I dug up the required quarters and went about my day.

Reading the news the next morning, I saw that it was International Women's Day.[4] As my husband and I headed out to meet his daughters, Alicia and Abby, for breakfast, I had a thought. *I should give those Susan B. Anthony coins to our granddaughters in celebration of the day.*

But first, some googling. I needed to refresh my knowledge of the achievements of Susan B. Anthony[5] so I'd be able to explain them in a way that would make sense to young girls.

At breakfast, my three-year-old granddaughter, Rowen, silently accepted her coins with a hug and a smile. My seven-year-old granddaughter, Ava, as predicted, was full of questions. "Why did she have to fight to vote? Haven't women always had the right to vote?" I had to explain to her that her great-grandmother Rose was born *before* women had the right to vote. She was *so* surprised. She could not comprehend that there was ever a time when women could not vote.

Once I explained it, she said, "Thank goodness for Susan B. and all of her friends!"

On the drive home, I thought about the journey of the past hundred years and Rose, my 103-year-old Italian mother-in-law. Born on February 22, 1916, a decade after Susan B. Anthony passed away, my mother-in-law was four years old when the Nineteenth Amendment[6] was ratified on August 18, 1920.

A momentous occasion in women's history—a history that was staring me in the face, figuratively and literally. Susan B. Anthony, in spirit, and Rose Agnes, in the living room asleep. Day by day, as history and the future collided in the here and now, the purpose of this book was becoming clearer.

And that was the end of Susan B. Anthony and me.

Or so I thought.

Later that afternoon, I was desperate for a break from writing the first draft of this book. For some reason, a certain book called out to me: *The Great Work of Your Life,* by Stephen Cope.[7] I had started reading it months ago, and then, well, life got in the way. But the book's message—to live your truth or sacred duty, your dharma—had encouraged me before. I guess I was searching for further inspiration.

I read about how Jane Goodall, Henry David Thoreau, and Robert Frost lived their dharma. All very inspirational and thought provoking. Then, in chapter six, I saw an eerily familiar name: Susan B. Anthony.

I almost dropped the book!

So, Ms. Anthony and I meet again. All within a twenty-four-hour period, and on International Women's Day, no less. Obviously, Susan B. Anthony had something to teach me—and my granddaughters.

I was ready to listen. Recently, while working on this book, I hit an internal wall. Deep down, I knew I had an important message to share with the world, but still, I was struggling with self-doubt. *What right did I have to live* large *and shout to the world the wisdom I know as truth? Why am I living small, like a kitten, when I have the strength of a lion trapped inside?*

Unfortunately, I know I am not alone in these struggles. I've been asked these same questions thousands of times after training a roomful of incredibly talented women. Why are *they* living so small when they have so much to offer the world? Why are *they* introducing themselves in a way that does *not* own the value they bring to the table?

Why is it so difficult for us all to accept a mere compliment, much less fully embrace the gifts we have to offer the world?

Susan B. Anthony[8] did indeed have a message that day.

The same sentence that described her life—"No great character in American history has been more ill-served by stereotyping, lame biographies, and stuffy hagiography"[9]— also describes women who pursue leadership positions today. One hundred years later, and here we are, fighting the same fight.

Did you know that Susan B. Anthony was not content to be a "good enough" public speaker?[10] She had to be great, and she became single-minded in her practice. She found a coach in her closest friend, Elizabeth Cady Stanton.[11] Everything— the way she dressed, the way she took care of herself, even the way she spoke—was reexamined. She poured her heart into doing whatever it took to become the powerful person she knew she *must* be to make a difference. Her passion[12] fueled her when the world would not.

Clarina Howard Nichols,[13] another women's rights advocate, wrote to Susan, "It is most invigorating to watch the development of a woman in the work for humanity: first, anxious for the cause and depressed with a sense of her own inability; next, partial success of timid efforts creating a hope; next, a faith; and then the fruition of complete self-devotion. Such will be your history."

Such will be your history, I whispered over and over again.

And then came the sentence that in my eyes changed Susan B. Anthony from a teacher to a sister: "Susan B. Anthony was determined not only to act on behalf of women, but to mobilize women to act for themselves."[14]

There it was. That was the reason I was writing this book. The. Exact. Same. Reason. *To mobilize women to act for themselves.* We hear you, sweet sister. We hear you.

THE GLASS CEILING IS ALSO A MIRROR

Once upon a time, not too long ago, a newly married couple was in their kitchen, enjoying each other's company as they prepared pot roast for dinner. The husband watched his wife cut off both ends of the pot roast before seasoning it and placing it in the oven. He thought it was odd—he had never seen anyone in his family do that. "Honey, why did you cut off both ends of the pot roast?"

She paused briefly and said, "I'm not sure. My mother always did."

At the next family gathering, the husband approached his mother-in-law. He explained what his lovely wife did and then asked why she cut the ends off the pot roast. His mother-in-law paused briefly and said, "My mother always did." The mystery continued.

Weeks later, the family gathered to visit their grandmother at her retirement community. The newlywed couple could not help but approach the grandmother, one hundred years old, born at the turn of the century. They explained the scenario and asked why she cut off the ends of the pot roast. The grandmother looked at her daughter and granddaughter. "Because my pan was too small!" she said.[15]

Subsequent generations behaved a certain way because of information they absorbed from observation—no big discussions. It was not written down as part of the recipe. It simply happened in the busyness of life. The unwritten rules snapped into place. The original problem—a too-small pan—was no longer an issue.

Here we are today, a world away from 1920. Or are we?

REWRITING THE NARRATIVE

Unlike Susan B. Anthony and the grandmother in the anecdote you just read, we live in a society where many people value women and actually want us at the table. We live in the era influenced by Sheryl Sandberg's book *Lean In*.[16] Sandberg is the chief operating officer of Facebook and founder of LeanIn.org,[17] a nonprofit organization that aims to inspire and support women in reaching their goals. It was exhilarating and empowering to see a woman with such influence change the conversation from what women can't do to what we can do. It was 2013, and I'd been working with numerous women's groups on many issues Sandberg's book brought to the forefront. The national dialogue that followed was invigorating and passionate and fueled a movement in much need of reenergizing.

But then the pushback began.[18] The collective conversation escalated into a debate about the role women played in leaning in versus the role organizations had in breaking the glass ceiling. The pendulum swung from empowering women to blaming the culture, the companies, the good ol' boys, and "the system." It reached a fever pitch in 2016 when, for the first time in history, a woman was a major party's nominee for president of the United States. We watched live, in color, as the ugliness of the campaign spilled toxicity into the culture. As the results of the election became a reality, tears rolled down the faces of hundreds of thousands of women—young and old. The heartbreak was real.

The ongoing collective narrative—women must overcome challenges; women are held down by "the system"; women must endure inaccurate perceptions—has run amok in the media. Yes, there have been great strides,[19] with more women running[20] for—and holding—elected office than any time in history,[21] yet much more remains to be done. Daily, the headlines, tweets, editorials, and updates are reinforcing a mindset that I believe is now standing in our way. What is the mindset? It is our view of *the Narrative*.[22]

The Narrative is the collective story line we have been listening to since birth—we've heard it from our families, from society, from the media, and from the workplace—regardless of where we live in the world. It has so infiltrated the culture that we have embraced these very distorted perceptions as truth—and nothing could be further from the truth. We might not be able to see it, but we sure can *feel* it. It's akin to a ton of bricks sitting on our shoulders, each one representing the boundaries drawn *for* us, the boxes created to *contain* us, and the beliefs suffocating our potential. It's as if every baby girl were given a book at birth on how to live, already half written *by someone else* with the unspoken expectation to simply "deal with it." We have another choice.

IS IT THE SYSTEM OR IS IT ME?

For far too long, we as women have been accepting the distorted messages driven by the Narrative as our personal issues when most of them—if not all—*are not ours.* The question of paramount importance as we navigate the next several years is: Is it the system, or is it me?

The Narrative (aka, the system) is rooted in a one-sided view of the world. Everything we have been taught is driven by history. When we see "history" for what it really is—*his* story—we finally begin to understand what has happened. Everything in the world has been developed through one lens—the original lens of *his*-story. Take a look:

> every rule,
> every law,
> every societal norm,
> every workplace practice,[23]
> every guideline,
> every compensation system,

every financial infrastructure,

every government,

and the list goes on and on.

As we shift into the space where we see the Narrative as a living, breathing entity, it will become clear when the Narrative is rearing its head—and, of course, fighting to stay alive. As women lead the shift to exploring new ways of doing almost everything, it is important to acknowledge the connections between the things we can see and the things we can't see. Things are rarely what they appear to be at first glance. It is imperative that we lay down the illusion of control that has been the hallmark of his-story and learn to respect that which we cannot see. We are inherently designed to dance with change.[24] This is our time to shine.

Once we choose to consciously embrace this deep intuitive intelligence, we can see the half-written book we were given at birth for what it is. The time has come for us to close that book and shift our focus to the beautiful, blank pages waiting for us. The time has come to write *her*-story.

What could the world look like if we paused long enough to see the world through a new lens of her-story? How would the world be different? Without the expectations that have been placed on our shoulders, without the judgment that has weighed us down, without the "shoulds" that we have been carrying for centuries, what would her-story look like? Is it even possible?

It absolutely is.

Draw inspiration from a news story that popped up in May 2018. It was on the news circuit for a few days—including CNN, the *New York Times*, and *Inc.*—but then quietly faded away. Its significance is worth bringing to light here because it is a powerful example of what her-story can look like once we are brave enough to jump out of the fishbowl and see it. Note how her-story naturally evolves into "*our story,*" as it is inherent to our design as women.

In May 2018, Rent the Runway cofounder and CEO Jennifer Y. Hyman announced that the company would offer the same benefits to all 1,200 of its employees. Everyone—from salaried C-suite executives to hourly warehouse workers—would have the same bereavement, parental, family sick leave, and sabbatical packages. "It's the right thing to do," said Hyman.

Hyman stumbled upon a startling revelation in spring 2018. "I realized I had set up a system where I just copied what best-in-class companies [did]," she told CNN's Poppy Harlow in an episode of *Boss Files.*[25]

She explained: "When you're founding a business, you take your cues on corporate culture from larger, already successful organizations. In America, some of the biggest companies have decided to handle the dual pressures of keeping costs down while retaining 'corporate talent' by ramping up benefits packages.

"But over the years, I began to reflect on how the system that I and others had constructed may have been perpetuating deep-seated social problems."

Hyman recounted the story of a seamstress who asked her if she could use the new paid family sick leave policy to take care of her daughter, who was having a baby via C-section the following week. She said the seamstress intended to quit her job so she could be home with her daughter, because she wouldn't have had the flexibility to take time for a medical procedure that wasn't her own.

"That's exactly what we created the new policy for," Hyman said. Despite the differences in contributions to the company, she explained, "My pregnancy is not any more important than the pregnancy of any single person who works at my company."

Pause and think about this for a moment.

Rent the Runway, a fashion industry pioneer that has grown from 50 employees to over 1,200, chose to also be a pioneer by redefining what the collective has accepted as a two-class-tier system of employees. Hyman's decision, supported by the board and company leadership, rewrote the Narrative around the way the system has "always been." A system originally created through the lens of his-story.[26] It is helpful at this point to refrain from judgment or slipping into the polarity of good versus bad. What this example brings to light is that the lens through which women see offers new possibilities of changing old realities.

Soon after announcing the new policy, Hyman coura-geously penned an opinion piece[27] for the *New York Times*, making her new policy public. "I had inadvertently created classes of employees and, by doing so, had done my part to contribute to American's inequality problem," she wrote.

She wrote that it is "incumbent that business leaders have to start acting like moral leaders," and she called on Wall Street to start having a "morality index."

"It's time for business leaders to step up and fulfill not only their fiduciary duty to shareholders but also their moral duty to society to treat every worker equally."

And she went one step further. Be inspired by the new reality she is "birthing" here:

"We have the power to create the kind of workplace culture we want. I want Rent the Runway to be an example of what a modern workplace should be—a leader in creating a more human workplace, where the heart is just as important as the head, and where we show that we care about each and every member of our team equally."

Can you feel the difference? We have all had a hand in continuing many of the practices and beliefs that were implemented under the old standards of success. It is time for a new story to be written, and women are uniquely suited to do so. Women are designed to create, and this ability to create is the source of our power.

Much like the energy of an atom, which creates everything,[28] you also have the power to create. Create a new life, a new movement, a new reality for yourself and for others. Once the power is ignited within, it cannot be contained. The power to shift the direction for the next generation lies inside each of us. As we consciously shift our focus, this new perspective has the potential to create a tsunami of change.

One woman—one sister—at a time.

Yes, there are larger societal issues that play a big role in the way women are treated, from the bedroom to the boardroom to the big screen. Yes, we absolutely must slay the dragon of disrespect every time it rears its head. Yes, we still have the Narrative to navigate, as we have one foot in the past and one foot in the future, straddling this space called the present. However, after many years spent coaching women, I have found that if our focus remains external, if we are always looking at what others are doing *to us*, we miss countless opportunities *for us*. The real power comes when we look within. Once you shift your focus internally, you will find that you can change your life.

Seeing through the Narrative and embracing powerful mindsets for our own life *first* is the key code that will unlock the collective shift we desire. When we change what we see in the mirror each day and the inner dialogue we have with ourselves, the collective power to create a world that truly values women will emerge. The answer does not solely lie outside ourselves. Therein lies the paradox.

Every time we pause, reflect, and consciously choose our direction, we create a new reality—individually and collectively. Perhaps you, too, will bravely find your Rent the Runway moment.

VICTIMHOOD, POWERLESSNESS, AND JUST: THE MEAN GIRLS OF YOUR MINDSET

Like the limiting collective narrative, personal mindsets can also unknowingly siphon our energy.

Victimhood. She was someone I knew all too well, but I had to say goodbye to her years ago. Victimhood seems like a friend at first, shifting your focus from what you need to do to what everyone else has done to you. It is comforting to have someone take your problems away, to give you a break from your own reality. That escapism is the lure of social media, our devices, and reality television. It is also the foundation for addictions to food, alcohol, drugs, and sex.

Much like other debilitating distractions, Victimhood can be mesmerizing. Empty promises of addressing the pain right now.

If they would do this or that, Victimhood whispers. *Others need to do their part.* At first, hanging out with Victimhood seems to be helping, until you meet her other friends. Powerlessness—nicknamed *"I can't!"*—is Victimhood's best friend. Powerlessness rears her ugly head when Victimhood begins to lose her luster. Drama, friend to both, waits in the shadows to stake her claim too.

"What do you mean you are tired?" Victimhood demands.

"Stay the course—they owe you."

Powerlessness chimes in, "How dare they do these things to you. How dare they ask so much of you!"

"Don't they know you are the victim here?" Victimhood says.

"Just keep doing what you are doing," a new voice appears. It's Just, perhaps the most dangerous girl of the group, for she can explain away anything.

If they could *Just* ...

I was *Just* trying to ...

I would be successful if they would *Just* ...

If they would *Just* remove the barriers ...

If they would *Just* stop judging me by their standards ...

I could earn more if I *Just* had a chance ...

If they could *Just* see how *their* bias is in our way ...

If they would *Just* show me more respect ...

I am *Just* a _____ (you fill in the blank: Jewish mother, girl from the Bronx, stay-at-home mom) ...

MY WATERSHED MOMENT

I'm living proof that it's possible to overcome limiting mindsets—conscious or unconscious. My watershed moment happened in 2002. My daughter, Heather, was five years old. I was one hundred pounds overweight. I read an article in a parenting magazine about how a parent's health was the biggest indicator of how healthy a child would be. I had flashbacks to all the struggles I'd had with weight, with a significant eating disorder and years of heartache, never feeling I was enough. I was unhappy with my personal life and trying to eat my way to happiness. While work was fulfilling, the demands caused significant hardships at home. I lived in a small town, and some days felt like I was living my own version of the movie *Groundhog Day.* I realized everything I was about—the good and the bad—was going to be passed down to my daughter.

Sobering, to say the least. Life changing, to say the best.

In that moment of insight, I committed to do whatever it took to change the course of *her life.* I did not want her to live through the constant pain I battled for decades. Like so many women, I could not muster up enough love *for myself* to make the changes needed; however, the love *for my daughter* provided a wellspring of strength. That love fueled me with determination and fortitude. In that galvanizing moment, everything changed—for me and for her.

> To my #sweetsisters who do not have children—know that I see you and cherish you for the treasure you are. We all have the power to birth new realities. Birthing children is only one of many ways we bring value to the world.

It was at that crossroads when I came face to face with generations of distorted thinking about women, about life, and about self-worth that had been passed down to me. Can you relate? Each generation's outlook on life had grown more distorted due to life's hardships.

I was dangerously close to passing along the previous generation's thinking to my daughter and sending her down a predictable path of hardship—a path where Powerlessness and Victimhood ruled the day.

It started with counseling to discover the root of my bulimia. I had taught systems thinking for seven years by then, so I knew my own beliefs (a.k.a. mental models) blinded me. *I did not know what I did not know.* First, I had to face the demons that ran through the family line. The emotional abuse, the alcoholism, the survival mindset, and the limited value of women—all placed on center stage for my review. Forced to grow up in poverty on the streets of Connecticut, my father's worldview was influenced by having to fight his way through life. He had an abusive father who eventually abandoned the family, leaving them to fend for themselves while starting a brand new family across the country, acting as if the old family never existed.

My mother was raised by a woman who was from a family of eight, working on a tobacco farm in North Carolina. Family was valued, and there were some good memories; however, survival was paramount to love—a pervasive undercurrent that permeated the lives of each family member. My mother was nineteen years old when she married my father. Each came into the marriage with less than what they deeply needed growing up. Two people wanting more than the other could provide, their marriage ending in a toxic divorce when I was thirteen years old.

Second, I had to consciously choose which mindsets I would release that were not healthy. This was an agonizing journey that brought me face to face with my responsibility for what I was willing to pass down to my daughter. I was the first in my family to obtain a four-year college degree, which ultimately led me on a solid path out of "survival" mentality. Then came the loss of almost one hundred pounds, changing my appearance.[29] I even got a new car. What seemed to be a simple midlife crisis was much more. It was a reclaiming of my identity. The changes on the outside reflected the significant metamorphosis inside.

I started to consciously choose to see the world through a different lens, asking many questions along the way. The good news is that life started to shift. The bad news is that I came face to face with the consequences of many choices I had made before this new Kim awakened. Back when I was a distorted version of myself, it was an awkward place to be. It was sobering to realize generations of confused thinking had led me to where I found myself. I slowly realized my external life was no longer a reflection of who I was inside. I could feel significant shifts on every level: cellular, soulful, emotional, spiritual. The gap between who I knew I was deep down and the persona the world knew as "Kim" was widening. The more it widened, the deeper I felt myself sinking into the mess.

I was in a crazy house, some of my own making, like a big, messy ball of twine all wound up. Powerlessness and Hopelessness were my constant companions. I unknowingly placed myself in a cage for over a decade, genuinely believing there was no hope.

When I was thirty years old, a decision was made for me: my lifelong dream of having lots of children was not going to happen. My heart splintered into a million pieces. That decision was the final nail in the coffin of the marriage, although it would take another thirteen years to hold the funeral. The desperation in the meantime almost drowned me. Yet the beautiful daughter I *was* given kept me afloat and inspired me to keep searching for the best version of myself.

The leverage for us as women? *We love others more than we love ourselves.* It is the unspoken epidemic of our time. When we become conscious of it, that epidemic can become our silent superpower.

WHICH PATH WILL WE CHOOSE?

As women, we are at a crossroads, a critical intersection between what was and what will be. We are facing an unprecedented window of opportunity this very moment. We are in the midst of an epicenter of change.[30]

We have two choices: Victimhood or victory. Powerless or powerful. We can take the path well traveled right now and buy into the Narrative that more people are *against* us than *for* us. We can choose to focus on negative statistics like the pay gap. After all, rarely does a week go by without the Narrative reminding us that men earn more than women. We can accept the notion that many seem to view our inherently female characteristics negatively. We can buy into the

Narrative's emphasis on inequity. Multiple workplace reports acknowledge how "inequities are taking a toll on women." And why wouldn't they? The sheer thought of tackling the beliefs that we are wronged in *so many* ways feels daunting. It leads many to feel powerless and to look "out there" for reasons why they're not succeeding to the level they're capable of. If we believe we are powerless, our language and our actions will reflect it—often unconsciously.

For women, individually and collectively, the question becomes: Which story is going to take root from this day forward? As we straddle the present—with one foot in the past and one foot in the future—what choice will we make? Will we choose to shift our focus to the power we *do* have, or will the Narrative, with all its negative perceptions that we (and our neurological pathways) have grown accustomed to, continue to take a front-row seat? Will we choose courageous leadership and stop repeating the old Narrative?

As a professional speaker and coach for C-level executives, I see the thirst for inspiring messages in women of all races and ages, across all levels of corporate leadership, spanning the globe. Recently, I had a conversation with a wildly talented, ambitious young professional. The topic of our conversation: Where could she find a female role model? Every single week, women around the world ask the same question. Where are our female role models for leadership?

However, there's a potential problem hidden in that question. As women, are we looking for a role model, or are we searching for a hero? Do we want someone to lead us or to save us? So many look up for the answer, down for the answer, to the right and to the left for the answer. Yet the answer lies within.

In our reflection is the answer we seek.[31]

We will never shatter the glass ceiling until each of us owns our piece of the Narrative.

HOW WE THINK ABOUT CHANGE

Young women are ... <u>significantly less confident</u> they can reach the top of the organization.

—2017 Women in the Workplace Report

"Women are less <u>optimistic</u> about their opportunity to advance: 1 in 4 women think that their gender has played a role in missing out on a raise, promotion, or chance to get ahead ..."

—2019 Women in the Workplace Report

In the 2016 Women in the Workplace Report,[32] a comprehensive look at women in corporate America published annually by LeanIn.org and McKinsey & Company, it was reported that women who hit the glass ceiling early are far less likely than men to be promoted from entry level to manager, and women hold less than 30 percent of roles in senior management. While highlighting the progress being made, the 2017, 2018, and 2019 reports echoed many of the same findings.

Why is that?

Why are many women not making that early jump—what the 2019 Women in the Workplace Report now refers to as the **"broken rung"**—in their careers? And why do they lose ground the more senior they become? This time, it is not about everyone else. It is about our misperceptions that distort what we see in the mirror every day. *Has the time come for us to consider that the glass ceiling is also a mirror?* By this, I mean that it is time for us to look at ourselves in the mirror and see that there are specific beliefs, assumptions, and internal mindsets also standing in our way. These mindsets don't show up in the new workplace surveys because many women themselves don't even realize that the mindsets are standing in the way. Why? It is unconscious, and the Narrative has convinced us otherwise.

May a global, collective conversation be ignited so that we are all more aware—for ourselves, for each other, and most importantly, for future generations. Much is at stake. As Melinda Gates emphatically states in her book, *The Moment of Lift*,[33] "When you lift up women, you lift up humanity."

COLLECTIVE VS. INDIVIDUAL CHANGE

The following explanation is based on a United States perspective; however, the thought process is what is important. I encourage you to think about the evolving story of women's empowerment in your own country as you read it. As a part of a global sisterhood, our stories are deeply connected.

The fight to which Susan B. Anthony and so many others dedicated their lives began in the mid-1800s and lasted more than fifty years. During that time, the only way the suffragettes were able to change the culture was through collective change.

Progress does not move in a simple, linear fashion. There are always unintended consequences—sometimes positive, sometimes negative. Being aware of these unintended consequences[34] invites us to take a second look so we don't become trapped in shifting the burden[35] unconsciously.

In 2020, the United States will celebrate the one hundredth anniversary of women earning the right to vote.[36] My 103-year-old mother-in-law, Rose,[37] lived with my husband and me for two years. As we cared for her, I was reminded of how long—and how short—one hundred years really is. So much has changed during her lifetime—and some things have stayed the same.

> Books that influenced my perception of Susan B. Anthony:
>
> *Penny Colman,* Elizabeth Cady Stanton and Susan B. Anthony: A Friendship That Changed the World *(New York: Henry Holt and Company, 2013).*
>
> *Ruth Rosen,* The World Split Open: How the Modern Women's Movement Changed America *(New York: Penguin Books, 2000).*

A centenarian whose parents emigrated from Sicily to Massachusetts in the early 1900s sees the world very differently. Rose's curiosity and wit remain as sharp as ever—throughout the day she listens to the radio, wanting to know the state of current affairs. When the Women's March took place in January 2017, she was baffled that so many women all over the world felt the need to march. After all, women are much better off now than they were then. "We all had to work hard in them days, regardless of how women were viewed," she said. "Why don't women today just focus on what they can do to better their situation? We never had time to march. There was too much to do!"

Here is how Rose—and many others—see the fight for equality:

But remember that part about unintended consequences?

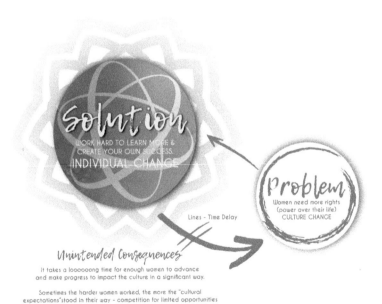

This is beginning to sound like the age-old argument of what came first, the chicken or the egg. In our case, it's what needs to come first: collective change or individual change?

Many women take for granted the freedoms they enjoy today, simply because they don't understand the significant battles previous generations fought to earn those freedoms. And yet, here we are, having some of the same conversations in 2020 that we had in 1920. Dissatisfaction with the status quo in the United States reached a tipping point on November 8, 2016, igniting and reviving the national women's movement. Attendance and participation in the Women's March[38] and International Women's Day[39] in 2017 crushed expectations. And the juxtaposition of two art installations in New York City—*Fearless Girl* and *Charging Bull*[40]—were reminders of the collective debate about the power of women.

Much of this was driven by one galvanizing moment: when in 2016 the dream of the first female president of the United States did not become reality. Regardless of which side you were on, we have a front-row seat to a growing dilemma for women's empowerment. Can we consider the possibility that Hillary Clinton's loss[41] was an unlikely gift for the women's movement? Without that loss—which galvanized millions of women to act—it's possible we might have been fooled into believing we made it. That we had achieved equity and fair treatment. The reality is that there was still much darkness in the system that needs to be brought to light.

The fallout from the case of Harvey Weinstein,[42] the Hollywood producer accused of sexual assault by dozens of women, and a multitude of other wrongdoings by others—like the Epstein saga[43]—that have been made public might not have come to light had the election turned out differently. Female journalists[44] across the globe are like warriors bringing awareness to these injustices, and it appears that we are still in the infancy of learning the full magnitude of what remains hidden. It may be helpful to think of light as information and darkness as lack of information. Think about being afraid of the dark as a child. Things seem much scarier when cloaked in darkness and you cannot see. When there is light, we have a chance to learn more and change as needed. We cannot heal our collective wounds until more light is brought to the darkness.

Is it possible that women are the catalyst for that healing?

Do we still need to come together collectively to drive the cultural change we want? *Yes!* Collective change drives cultural change, and cultural change drives even more collective change. Let the #MeToo movement[45] serve as one example of the impact and importance of collective change.

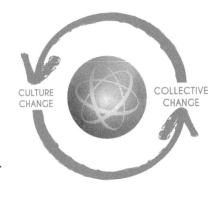

In one hundred years, our culture *has* changed; however, it hasn't changed *enough*. We can all agree on that, but can we agree on how to get where we really want to be? This much is certain: we can't keep using the same techniques that women used in the early 1900s. Yet it seems that some are using the same old playbook. If it worked once, it should work again, right? Wrong—the system has changed. Let me explain.

COLLECTIVE *AND* INDIVIDUAL CHANGE

Think of it like parenting. New parents follow a certain set of rules and use specific skills with their baby. As the baby becomes a toddler, parents change the rules and their approach. No one in their right mind would use the same

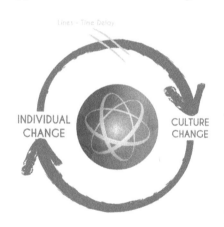

parenting skills for a toddler and a teenager. Why? Because the two are entirely different. Ask any parent: raising a teenager is very different than raising a toddler. Fortunately, it is "easy" to adjust because the parent sees

the child grow up. **The women's movement has grown up too.** It now requires additional insight and skills. Collective change is *not* the only tool in our tool kit. Individual change is also a key factor.

The same issue exists here as before. It takes a long time for individual change on its own to drive cultural change. Cause and effect are far removed in space and time: we are still influenced by the mindsets from the generations before us *and* we have the power to affect future generations one hundred years from now. It is important to truly grasp the interdependence[46] of the actions of those who came before us and those who will come after us. The future that unfolds depends on the choices we make now—day by day, decision by decision.

Recently, I had an eye-opening conversation with a millennial woman, one of the many professionals I asked for feedback on this book. "Why do you even mention Susan B. Anthony?" she asked. "She's not relevant to today's world."

Wow. *Not relevant?* Even if this woman never cared to vote in her life, Susan B. Anthony made so much more possible for all of us. For me, her reaction was a startling reminder of the short-term focus most of us have. This thirty-three-year-old woman was blinded by what she couldn't see, even though it was right in front of her. I realized that I needed to do a better job of connecting the dots.

If it were not for the actions of many brave and committed women like Susan B. Anthony—and others like Ella Baker (a civil rights activist),[47] Sojourner Truth (an abolitionist and women's rights activist),[48] and Alice Walker (a writer and activist)[49]—over one hundred years ago, we might still be dealing with the issues they did. Can you imagine not being allowed to stay overnight in a hotel alone[50] or speak in public without fear[51]? Can you picture a life in which all your assets became your husband's when you married? And can you believe that those assets included your children? In comparison to *that* type of life, having conversations about shattering the glass ceiling would be a luxury.

Thankfully, because women before us fought these obstacles, many of us—though not all—live in a different reality than they did. We are free to have conversations about gender differences, the glass ceiling, sexual harassment, and rewriting the Narrative. But conversations can take us only so far; we have reached a tipping point where collective change is not the only answer.

So, what is the answer? Balance.

Both collective change *and* individual change are needed. Without the other to provide balance, the pendulum swings too far to one side. Think of this balance like a pair of glasses. If we had only one lens,[52] what we saw would be distorted. A clear image emerges *only* when we look through both lenses.[53]

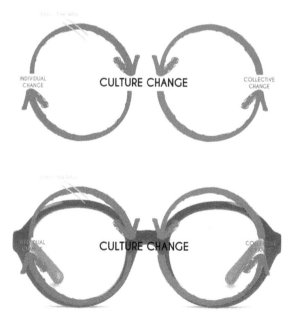

HOW WE THINK AND FEEL ABOUT
GENDER DIFFERENCES

Dr. Matthew Price[54] is a respected pioneer in media psychology and applied behavioral neuroscience and former vice president of global media and technology for Nielsen Consumer Neuroscience. He thought I'd be interested in the emerging field of sentiment analysis,[55] which, broadly speaking, uses artificial intelligence to determine the attitude of an audience with respect to a select topic.

Dr. Price introduced me to Centiment,[56] a research company doing groundbreaking work in the field. Its program uses artificial intelligence to analyze over one million data points, including world news, global trends, and social media in real time, to calculate the emotions surrounding any topic. Micah Brown,[57] Centiment's founder and CEO, took a few of the topics covered in this book—the glass ceiling, gender bias, women in the workplace, and gender equality—and ran a sentiment analysis on these topics.

The results, especially in the social media sphere, shed light on the worldwide impact of the Narrative. These were the general emotions surrounding these issues, in order of strength:

1. Anger

2. Disgust

3. Sadness

Worldwide, the general vibe toward the topic of gender differences is overwhelmingly negative. Although the field of sentiment analytics is still in its infancy, these results offer compelling insight into not only the language women are using to discuss these issues but also the *emotions* behind their words.

In addition to this sentiment data, when it comes to the current state of affairs, there are three cognitive biases at work as well. The first is the bandwagon effect:[58] the more people who hold a belief, the greater the probability that we will each adopt the belief. The second is the availability heuristic.[59] With this bias, we tend to place too much value and importance on the information that is available to us. Each week a newspaper headline, a blog post, or a media interview is drawing us into the Narrative, albeit sometimes unconsciously.

The third bias is anchoring,[60] the tendency to rely too heavily on the first piece of information offered when making decisions.

Is it possible that women, anchored by the constant, repetitive cultural and gender stereotypes they face daily, are unconsciously agreeing with the general belief that women are less capable in some way or that the challenges we face are insurmountable?

Dr. Price believes it is quite possible: "I spend a lot of time studying the nature of reality and the human experience. I try to objectively explain how our worldviews and collective consciousness meld to become what we generally agree is reality. But our reality is nothing more than a social contract wherein each of us, men and women alike, agree to certain norms and expectations. To fulfill that contract, we have an unspoken responsibility to each other to find in ourselves balance and equality; only then can we hope to expect the same from others." This is powerful insight from someone who specializes in interpreting the messages we collectively receive every day. The drumbeat of what we can't see is so loud we can no longer hear it.

LOOKING AT GENDER DIFFERENCES DIFFERENTLY

Perhaps to lead the Narrative away from Victimhood and toward victory, we are being invited to think about gender differences differently. Although by no means a comprehensive review of all the literature on these topics, three recent studies offer insight and advice. And while their findings may not be conclusive, they certainly are eye opening.

DOWNPLAY THE DIFFERENCE

A July 2017 Columbia Business School study[61] focused on how the way women discuss gender can affect their workplace confidence and behavior. The conclusion: Gender blindness (the belief that gender differences should be downplayed) is a more adaptive strategy for increasing female workplace confidence than gender awareness (the belief that gender differences should be celebrated).

It appears that decreasing the focus on gender might be a more adaptive ideology for closing the confidence gap and helping women take action to shape their career outcomes.

POWER AND GENDER IDENTIFICATION

In a July 2016 study,[62] professors at Yale and New York University examined how high-power mindsets affect gender identification. They found a direct link between holding power and lower group identification: women who were made to feel powerful reported lower levels of gender identification. Interestingly, this effect was not found in men.

Such results can help explain Carly Fiorina's response to becoming the first female CEO of Hewlett-Packard in 1999: "I was completely unprepared for the amount of attention that was paid to my gender ... I had so long ago stopped thinking about myself as a woman in business and thought about myself as a businessperson who happened to be a woman."

HOLLYWOOD ISN'T HELPING

A study published in Organizational Dynamics *in 2013 reviewed over one hundred films featuring managerial and professional women in leading or supporting roles to identify specific biases in how such women are portrayed on film.*[63] *Overwhelmingly, researchers found that media does not "frame" women in positive or empowering ways. The portrayal of professional women is frequently represented as deeply flawed or wanting, while the depictions of women's attempts to advance professionally are generally less than flattering. In their conclusion, the researchers agreed: "As we face the ongoing conundrum of the glass ceiling, the role of the media in perpetuating this problem deserves further exploration and critique. Films, along with commercials, television shows, and online content, communicate socio-cultural understandings that shape viewers' perceptions of reality, in particular their* **mental models** *of appropriate gender roles."*

Is it possible that women have unknowingly become partners in keeping the Narrative alive?

The entire story line we have all bought into around the glass ceiling—which wasn't a common phrase until 1986, when the *Wall Street Journal* used it[64]—is a societal problem.

Remember, these studies and countless others are all influenced by the Narrative tap dancing on the collective subconscious. It is helpful to think of the Narrative as a person—a living, breathing entity that draws strength from our need to seek heroes and place blame. Blinded by what we can't see, the Narrative is counting on us to remain unaware. What if we consciously placed the Narrative to the side and, shining a bright light on that which is lurking in the shadows, started a fresh page?

CORPORATIONS CAN'T DO IT ALONE

Despite numerous workplace reports, growing diversity initiatives, and increased awareness, the sobering reality is that corporations can't do it alone. The mindsets fueling the Narrative are being absorbed—like the pot roast lesson—long before we enter the workplace. This is a major 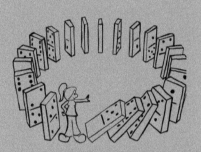 *issue contributing to what is now referred to as the "broken rung" highlighted in the 2019 Women in the Workplace Report. In our short-term-driven world, let us pause long enough to understand that cause and effect is far removed in space and time.*

Having a greater understanding of how the workplace works is but one chapter in a much larger story and is crucial to our ability to change the culture. There are a multitude of unintended consequences to our inner dialogue as women, for ourselves, our children, and the young people we mentor. May we be brave as we consider the unspoken messages being passed down from generation to generation.

FROM MEAN GIRLS TO SWEET SISTERS

No one was more surprised than I to find a universal set of beliefs standing in our way that transcends age, race, culture, economic status, or leadership position. It had to be more complicated, didn't it? Sadly, that is a myth too many have bought into. There is great power in Simplicity. Become friends with her on this journey. Simplicity feels lighter, more inviting, and nobler. A true friend.

Earlier, I introduced you to Victimhood, one of the mean girls who can inhabit your mind. Victimhood, you see, tried to befriend me quite early in life: I was born with a significant hearing impairment. *You have a disability!* Victimhood whispered. Fortunately, I was also born an optimist, so instead of seeing a devastating disability, I found an inspiring teacher. To effectively manage everyday life, I learned how to "hear" much more than what people said—I listened to *what people didn't say.*

That ability led me to Truth, a brilliant personality who has since become a soul mate. On this journey called life, Truth has introduced me to Power, Strength, and Hope. They are quite a crew—endearing, fun, creative, and courageous. Together, they led me to the Sisterhood of Seven: Seven Stories, Seven Mindsets.

They are all standing by, arms open wide, with an invitation to rewrite the Narrative. The Sisterhood of Seven will introduce the most common beliefs unconsciously standing in our way and, more importantly, will show us how to shift those beliefs so we each can discover the power within.

It starts with you and me. Right here. Right now.

#reWritetheNarrative

MEET THE
SISTERHOOD

After training and coaching tens of thousands of leaders, I learned that the key to transformational change is shifting your individual mindset. These leaders would invest their energy in learning new skills, trying different techniques, and giving themselves a daily pep talk to overcome their fears and failures. These efforts would help, but not in a dramatic way or not for very long.

Why? Because inevitably, the deeply held mindsets and beliefs of these leaders would bubble up, unconsciously at times, and mitigate any progress.

To truly understand the power of an individual's mindset (including your own), it's helpful to look at the concept of mental models. Mental models are the lenses through which we see the world. They're the specific set of glasses we wear to interpret everything. They're not right or wrong; they simply are. We have mental models about everything: the way kids should be raised, the way the company should be run, the way governments should be led, or how we should age. Mental models are extremely powerful.

The danger of mental models is that we often operate from them—unconsciously. We don't even realize they are influencing our decisions. In fact, mental models drive the entire notion of confirmation bias, which is the tendency to search for, interpret, and recall information in a way that confirms our existing beliefs. Even if we are surrounded by facts showing us other ways, we stick with what we already know.

I see it happen to leaders every single week. They are so entrenched in their world that they can no longer *see* clearly. Even worse, they don't even know they can't see clearly. The greatest crisis we face today is a lack of awareness. Contributing to this lack of awareness is an unwillingness to respectfully embrace the notion that we each see the world through a very different lens—perspective. This lack of understanding is driving us to seek what we believe is THE answer. Capital T. Capital H. Capital E. THE answer is an illusion. It does not exist. Clarity comes from acknowledging there is "an" answer. "An" answer takes on more power when we consider it within the context of the system that has a life of its own. The system evolves, changes, and adapts much like nature does. Is it possible that nature offers us wisdom in the arena of leadership—personally and professionally? Is it possible our ability to discover the power within is embedded within our DNA of thought? I believe it is quite possible.

We now understand that DNA is a genetic code that determines the characteristic of a living thing (a.k.a. system). The information stored within DNA provides the blueprint for hereditary material—the information that is passed on to the next generation. We recognize the double helix as the symbol of this amazing discovery. My work has proven to me that mental models are the highest leverage for change—individually and collectively. I have started to wonder if the double helix is shaped like a miniladder to serve as an invitation for us all to climb higher and see our world through a different perspective.

More and more, we are looking to DNA for answers in life.[65] We gain insight into our lineage with a DNA ancestry kit.[66] We map our health and wellness with a DNA health kit.[67] The power of DNA to change the way we understand the world is in its infancy. New discoveries are coming to the forefront,[68] showing that we are not trapped by our DNA. That each cell holds a potential reality passed down through generations, but our individual lives can determine the outcome. Building upon this reasoning, can we consider the possibility that inherent within our design, we have the ability to shift so we may tap into potential that we have not consciously acknowledged yet?

The Sisterhood is bringing awareness to this possibility so each of you can discover your personal power and live your fullest life. Breathe in the magnitude of this realization. We have the power to create our reality within each present moment. Thought creates, and that is wisdom worth building on.

So how do we start to shift to unlocking a new reality? It takes three steps.

Pause – Reflect – Choose

STEP 1. PAUSE

It takes conscious effort to pause long enough to catch the automatic thought process and shift it in a different direction. Between every action and reaction, there is a space, and in that space is the opportunity for change. It is your pivot zone—it's where we pause long enough to stop ourselves from the automatic reaction.[69] In that space we embrace awareness.

STEP 2. REFLECT **AND ZOOM OUT**

Once we catch that automatic thought, we reflect and zoom out. We consciously choose to see things from a different perspective by going up on the mountaintop. We ask ourselves why. Why did I say that? Why did I do that? Do I really believe that, or is something else influencing me? Am I reacting consciously or unconsciously? What is it that I am not saying out loud? Is it possible that someone else's narrative is coming out of my mouth?

The theory is if you ask why seven times, you will eventually find the truth. You will likely discover that something happened in your past that your mind took a snapshot of. You unconsciously placed that snapshot into your mental folder called "This Is the Way Things Are." Without knowing it, you've been placing things in that folder your entire life. You collected some items from your family. You added a few things from teachers and bosses.

Any time something out of the ordinary happened, you placed it in a different folder titled "Never Allow This to Happen Again." Much like a filing cabinet, these mental folders eventually reach a point where they're overflowing with stuff. The thing about our mental filing cabinet is that we rarely pause long enough to ask which files should stay and which should go. We simply keep filing stuff until our brain is overflowing with mindsets (a.k.a. mental models) that have outgrown their usefulness. The system grows up—like a teenager—but our mindsets stay the same—like a toddler.

The Sisterhood says, "Sisters, it's time to clean out the files. There are too many beliefs standing in the way, individually and collectively."

STEP 3. CHOOSE

We have the power to choose. We really do, although that power is often buried under a lot of shoulds, don'ts, and can'ts—all that the world has stuffed into our mental folders. The Sisterhood wants to wipe away all that has blinded us from possibility. It is important to remember that small actions have a big impact. The changes the Sisterhood asks from us will happen day by day, decision by decision. It's not one huge shift—it's hundreds of small shifts taking place each day to each of us that will eventually create a tsunami of change in the way we think and live.

What are the most common mental models showing up for women around the world? What do they look like in daily life? What do they sound like?

It's time for you to meet the Sisterhood of Seven.

Each of the seven sisters represents a mental model, hidden deep down inside, that often unconsciously influences our actions. At first glance, some of these mental models may seem obvious. Others may sound shocking. To be honest, I was surprised to see some of them myself. My first reaction was disbelief. No way. We have come too far! We can't still be thinking this way. But then I did my own research. I started testing each mental model, one by one, with the thousands of women with whom I've worked around the world—across industries, races, ages, and backgrounds, and across cultures, leadership positions, and experience. And my results consistently led me to one conclusion: like it or not, the Sisterhood is right.

Don't be surprised if a time or two you feel uncomfortable while reading—accept it as a signal you are knocking on the door of a personal breakthrough. Simply breathe deeply. Thank your brain for alerting you to the feeling. Keep reading. Choose to be brave, and good things will happen.

TRACKING THE SISTERHOOD

To avoid the inevitable judgment that comes with polarized declarations—good versus bad, right versus wrong—the mindsets of the Sisterhood are explained using a traffic light analogy. As each sister reveals herself to you, it is important to remember that change takes place on a continuum.

Red zone—STOP and become aware.

What is not being said in this moment? Are you on automatic pilot? Is there a seed of powerlessness that is seeking acknowledgment? On the journey through life, the toughest parts are the intersections. There is always a choice. Only too many of us are blowing past the intersections in a hurry, missing the opportunity waiting for us to pivot.

Many are not inclined to change until we feel pain. It could be the pain of not feeling well that drives us to change our eating habits. Perhaps it is the pain of enduring a difficult marriage. Or maybe it is the pain of not receiving the job or promotion we worked so hard for. Whatever the situation, pain is often the catalyst for change.

Why is it, though, that one person can face a painful situation and break free, yet another person stays trapped? Why can one woman face a divorce and go on to create a new life full of joy, while another woman's divorce becomes the defining moment of her life and keeps her spinning in a downward spiral? The difference in these women and their reactions is perspective, and it's the gift pain gives us:

Path to
Another way;
Invitation for a
New direction

Yellow zone—SLOWLY move forward.

Consider an internal shift that will allow your light to shine brighter by taking a small step forward—in a different direction. Embrace the power you have shown in the yellow zone.

Green zone—Green means GO.

The green zone is where the freedom is. Go full speed ahead to unleash the best side of yourself. Freedom is beckoning to you in the green zone, which will allow you to discover the power within. Think of the Sisterhood as a bridge to freedom. Freedom from the self-sabotaging behaviors in your way. Freedom from the limitations the world has placed on you. Freedom from the limitations you place on yourself.

Everyone responds to the Sisterhood differently. For some women, simply becoming aware of the mindset will be incredibly freeing, and they will automatically shift—almost like a light switch; however, most need a little more time to internalize the shift. Be patient with yourself. The pace at which you cycle through the mindsets depends on the amount of pain in your life, conscious or unconscious. There is no right or wrong way; there is only *your* way. Every win for yourself in breaking free from these illusions is a win for you and your sisters.

If it were so easy to make the changes, we would have already done so. Think back to the fishbowl analogy. The reality is we have been swimming with the Narrative for so long that it can be challenging to see at first glance. This is where the Sisterhood of Seven comes in. Each sister has a message. Many relate to more than one sister at a time.

Why do they call themselves a sisterhood? Because the mindsets will feel familiar to you, like family. You have danced with these sisters at their best, and you have danced with them when they are the most challenging. As we each straddle the present the Sisterhood of Seven is here to bring light to that which is still standing in the way. Remember that each belief served you at one time in your life, so don't invite Judgment along for the ride. Judgment is a black-belt ninja at perpetuating the Narrative—the very one we want to free ourselves from. This journey is about consciously and purposefully making choices. Day by day. Decision by decision.

Each sister will be revealed one at a time, but here is a look at where we are going. See page 233 for a complete chart, or download it at YourLionInside.com. Carry it with you as a tool on your journey to live your fullest life. Think of the inspiration guide like a decoder for a treasure map, only this time the treasure is YOU.

		▲	
🫀 KARI	THE KARI STORY I expect perfection	▲	I believe DONE is better than perfect	I AM enough
💎 RANEE	THE RANEE STORY I have to meet all demands	▲	I CAN say no	Here is what I am willing to do
🌸 GABRIELLA	THE GABRIELLA STORY I need permission/approval	▲	I TRUST my own decisions	I can move forward in confidence
⚫ DARSHA	THE DARSHA STORY I should accept what is said *(or done)*	▲	I CAN pause, reflect and choose	I choose to rewrite the narrative
🦅 AVALENE	THE AVALENE STORY I'm not qualified enough	▲	I AM the right one for the opportunity	There is enough for me AND you
✳ JALILA	THE JALILA STORY If I work hard enough, I will be rewarded	▲	I can advocate and CARE for myself	I own and articulate my value
〰 NIKKI	THE NIKKI STORY I'm okay in the background	▲	I AM powerful and that's okay	My power is MUCH needed in this world

THE KARI STORY

I EXPECT PERFECTION

Kari is a busy mompreneur—a business owner who is actively balancing the role of mom and entrepreneur. A seventeen-year marketing veteran, Kari owns two businesses; has three children (two under the age of four); and has a passion for cooking, her clients, and generally overextending herself. Her most recent business, a dating coaching company, has been featured in *Forbes* and *Business Insider* and on several network news programs. She is a wise soul with big ideas to change the world. Her genuine, no-nonsense spirit endears her to clients. Her ambition, thirst for big ideas, and willingness to drive results is what keeps this woman on the go.

"I have little kids who hate to eat—and I *love* to cook and feed others. I call myself a 'social feeder,'" says Kari. "So, when our neighborhood held a potluck, I was all in. The prospect of having a whole group to cook for was exhilarating. Adults! People who would appreciate what I had to offer!"

Digging through an extensive recipe collection, Kari carefully selected a few of her best and set to work. The big day arrived, and as so often happens, it ended up being a little crazier than expected. Her parents randomly stopped by for a short visit. At the last minute, her husband decided to go fishing, which translated into no one available to help watch the crazy kiddos. And before she even got to work making all the food she had promised, she had to stop by a friend's baby's birthday party (with an appropriate gift, of course), *and* she still had to run around in search of a few gourmet, hard-to-find ingredients for her fabulous recipes. Oh, and raspberries still needed to be gathered from the garden (her girls had already eaten her first harvest earlier in the day).

Kari was stretched thin, to say the least. More accurately, she was stressed, exhausted, and overcommitted. Yet she had grand plans to create a magnificent frozen masterpiece. What she didn't count on: her ice cream machine not working.

Here was her Facebook post the next morning:

"Friends, I am tired and it's my own dang fault. When it comes to feeding others, I go way overboard and it's going to kill me one of these days. Last night our neighborhood had a potluck party. Instead of being a normal person, I had to make 2 gallons of homemade, homegrown raspberry ice cream and 5 gallons of HOMEMADE root beer. The root beer was easy BUT it took time to track down all the ingredients (root beer extract, dry ice, etc.—things not generally laying around in my pantry).

"On top of that, I also volunteered to make the meat for the party. Naturally, I went with ribs, so think about all the prep time there too. Remember how I run two businesses and have tiny, crazy children too?

"Bottom line, I LOVE hosting things and feeding people but I need an intervention. Seriously though, next time I am going to bring some chips.

"I'm gonna go nap now."

LIFE WITH KARI IN THE RED ZONE

"I expect perfection."

This is the kind of language you will hear when in the red zone with Kari:

- "It will take just a little extra time, really."

- "I am just trying to make sure everyone is taken care of."

- "I just can't help myself."

- "I'm sorry; I have not had time to … "

- "Sure, I can do that."

This is the energy—often unspoken and unconscious—behind Kari in the red zone. Circle those that resonate with you:

- Purity of heart (albeit misguided at times)
- Never good enough
- Angst
- Striving

- Going the extra mile at a personal price
- Never ending
- Exhausted
- Apologetic

LOOKING FARTHER DOWN THE ROAD

Here are some unintended consequences to consider when we spend time with Kari in the red zone:

- **We're driven to extremes.** Perfection is an illusion, yet the pursuit of it still shows up in people, places, and circumstances. Think about Pinterest, endless photo-editing apps, and the quest for the ultimate image to share with the world.

- **We are never at peace in the present moment.** The time building up to an event is filled with anxious energy to do everything just right. The time after the event is filled with longing for what you had hoped to do. Not to mention, you miss enjoying the event itself because you're not living in the present moment.

- **We waste time on things that won't matter in the long run.** The expectation for perfection adds unnecessary pressure to relationships and creates unrealistic expectations. All of this leads to exhaustion once again, robbing those close to you of the best you have to offer.

- **Our children learn to focus on everyone and everything else.** Kari is very close to the next sister, Ranee, who strives to meet all demands. Our daughters internalize our desperate quest to make things just right, creating a never-ending cycle.

- Is it possible that our expectations for perfection **set the stage for our sons to expect perfection in the future**? Are we unknowingly teaching our sons that women *will do it all*, a cycle that shows up in the future at work *and* at home?

LIFE IN THE GREEN ZONE

"I am enough."

This is the kind of language you will hear when in the green zone with Kari:

- "It would be great to do *X*, but not this time."

- "All is well."

- "I've done enough already."

- "I am going to take care of myself this time."

- Silence—because no words are needed.

This is the energy—radiating from the inside out—behind Kari in the green zone:

- Peaceful

- Calm

- Deep wisdom and understanding

- Breath of fresh air

- Accepting and in the *now*

- Shift from *doing* to *being*

- No longer has anything to prove

THE REST OF THE STORY: A FOLLOW-UP CONVERSATION WITH KARI

When did your aha moment happen that motivated your Facebook post?

My aha moment came when I was sitting at the party. Everyone was having a great time—except me. I was flustered that the ice cream was melting. People were not actually going to get to taste it and therefore praise me for it. I realized the next morning, as I was exhausted, sore, and grumpy, that my desire to serve others was really self-serving.

Did you realize perfection was influencing you unconsciously?

Here's the thing—I would have never said I was a perfectionist. I rebel against the very concept! I have three kids—have you seen my house? I've learned my lessons around perfection paralysis in the past. I wouldn't consider myself or my motivations coming from perfectionism. Whenever I've met people who are perfectionists, it seemed like a condition they had. I didn't realize perfectionism can show up in circumstances!

What was your biggest takeaway from this experience?

"Next time I would rather be fed than dead."

#theKaristory #myKari

KARI

THE MEANING OF THE LOGO

See the heart as a prism. It offers different perspectives—a chance to see the same thing through a fractal imaging process that is difficult to interpret through a single dimension. Think of a diamond shining brilliantly. The same object angled in the light provides different colors and awe-inspiring experiences. The fullness of the spectrum is quite powerful. Every time you look, you can see something new. When the light is not shining through, it does not mean the colors are not there. It simply means there is a temporary dimming of the light. Trust that the jewel is still valuable. Deep down, you know the light is always there and it is ready to illumine the way.

INSPIRATION ON THE
JOURNEY TO FREEDOM

AFFIRMATIONS

- Perfection is an illusion.

- I will pause long enough to ask, "Is this really necessary?"

- I was made to be me—why be anyone else?

- Today, I am enough.

- The world needs me to be me.

SONGS TO MOTIVATE YOU

- *Strength, Courage & Wisdom,* by India.Arie
- *A Rose Is Still a Rose,* by Aretha Franklin
- *Q.U.E.E.N.,* by Janelle Monáe
- *Beautiful,* by Christina Aguilera
- *Born This Way,* by Lady Gaga[70]

MOVIES AND BOOKS TO ENERGIZE YOU

- *The Gifts of Imperfection: Let Go of Who You Think You're Supposed to Be and Embrace Who You Are and Dare to Lead: Brave Work. Tough Conversations. Whole Hearts,* by Brené Brown
- *Moana*
- *Wild: A Journey from Lost to Found,* by Cheryl Strayed
- *The Ultimate Risk,* by Tara L. Robinson[71]

TRUE STORIES TO INSPIRE YOU

- *"Untangling the Roots of Dominican Hair" at GreatBig-Story.com*
- *"Why My Gray Hairs Make Me Happy," from The Stay At Home Chef on YouTube.com*
- *"Mel Robbins—Outsmart Your Brain," at Goalcast.com*
- *"SuperSoul Short: Kidada Jones, School of Awake," from OWN on YouTube.com.*[72]

HEALING MODALITIES TO ASSIST YOU

- *Peace and Calming oil, by Young Living—This blend is helpful in times of stress and balance and contentment.*

- *Peace and Calm also comes from working with: lavender, Roman chamomile, rose, ylang ylang, and cedarwood. Serenity is a lovely blend by DoTERRA.*

- *Magnolia—Can reduce feelings of anxiety.*

- *Flower essence: Black-eyed Susan—I AM Me.*

REFLECTION

As you read about Kari, what resonated with you? When has the expectation for perfection stood in your way? How does it show up in your world?

_____

_____

_____

_____

What are some unintended consequences of the expectation of perfection?

_____

_____

_____

_____

How do you feel[73] about the three simple words: "I am enough"?

_____

_____

_____

_____

THE RANEE STORY

I HAVE TO MEET ALL DEMANDS

Energetic and spunky, Ranee is a deep thinker with loads of creativity and ambition. She earned an MBA from a prestigious business school (where she was student council vice president of a college with thirty-five thousand students, a leader in her sorority, and a top academic) and was now working her way up through management positions with a key player in the healthcare industry.

She had boundless energy—an enviable trait, admirable as well, since she also had an equally energetic nine-month-old daughter. However, all that energy was misdirected. Ranee was always going one hundred thousand miles per hour but not in any specific direction. Instead, she was doing everything in every area of her life: professional and personal.

As one coworker said, "I want Ranee to know that she does not have to say *yes* to everything!"

Feedback from superiors suggested that Ranee "needed to harness her energy. She is very passionate, but it can be overwhelming. She has a hard time learning to 'wait' for the right time."

Interestingly, additional feedback about Ranee was that "she didn't look the part" of an executive at the next level. Fair enough. But the commentary continued: "She is not able to spend much time on herself after having a baby." Sounds like the Narrative was working its toxic ways, doesn't it?

Can you imagine a sleepless new father receiving a similar assessment? This serves as a reminder: as you work on the mindsets of your internal world, the Narrative is still alive and well in the external world.

Still, the higher-ups saw much potential in Ranee. They admired her ability to motivate others, her openness to learn, and her willingness to do whatever it took to climb the ladder. "She brings a lot of positive to the table ... we see a long runway with her."

But somehow, despite her effort and output, was it possible Ranee was standing in her own way?

A few years ago, she was at company headquarters, working as one of the main architects of a $100 million deal. She had established quite a reputation for herself as being dangerously creative when it came to creating big deals that required new ways of thinking. "This deal was particularly important because it affected some of our largest clients,"

Ranee said. "Everyone was pressed for time and ideas, as the pressure was on to reach the project goals on deadline."

The large team started early in the morning. Midday, a male manager, who was sitting next to Ranee, said, "It's almost lunchtime, gang. I think we need to order."

Immediately, almost instinctively, Ranee jumped up and began taking lunch orders for the entire group. She remembers the day clearly because it offered a lesson she never forgot. "I was driving to Subway to fetch lunch for this room full of men and crying the whole way," she says. "I was in disbelief. After all these years and *all this hard work*, I was the person picking up lunch. It felt awful. I felt awful."

Her mind was racing. She thought about how little value she must provide to this group. The story she created in her head went downhill from there. It did not help that she had just returned from maternity leave. She began to wonder if maybe she wasn't needed while she was gone. Maybe she had not been as valuable as she thought. For days, she made herself crazy thinking about things she could have done to avoid "being the person who gets lunch." It felt so powerless. She made her husband crazy too. Ranee was consumed by thinking of ways to muster up enough strength next time to say, "Yes, I am hungry too. Let's have someone get us lunch." Why didn't she do that?

Fast-forward one year—same company, another big deal. Ranee had since been promoted to the same level as the manager who had suggested lunch. And once again, he was sitting next to her at the meeting. She had just flawlessly delivered a strong idea that had heads nodding around the room. The manager turned to her and said, "That is really smart, Ranee." To which she quickly responded, "Thank you. I guess I can do more than get lunch." Confused, he asked what she meant. She told him about being the one to get lunch the year before. He laughed and said, "I was just hungry. I meant *someone* should get us lunch. I didn't mean you needed to be the one to do it."

| I have to meet all demands | ▶ | I CAN say no | ▶ | Here is what I am willing to do |

LIFE WITH RANEE IN THE RED ZONE

"I have to meet all demands."

This is the kind of language you will hear when in the red zone with Ranee:

- "I'll do it!"

- "I can take care of that—no problem."

- "I will be glad to do that," *sigh*.

- "I have a lot on my plate, but I guess *one more thing* won't matter."

- "I'm *just* trying to make it easier on everyone else."

This is the energy—often unspoken and unconscious—behind Ranee in the red zone. Circle those that resonate with you:

- Pressured
- Busyness is a distractor (from silence, life's problems, etc.)
- Victimhood

- Tethered to Kari and her worldview of perfection
- Taken advantage of
- Resentful at times
- Powerless

LOOKING FARTHER DOWN THE ROAD

Here are some unintended consequences to consider when we spend time with Ranee in the red zone:

- **We spin ourselves into exhaustion.** Many times, the pressure on our shoulders is self-induced. The opportunity? Allow space for others to respond first. We don't have to race to save everyone all the time.

- **A vein of resentment builds over time.** The outcome is predictable. We will eventually explode or implode: an emotional breakdown, a physical illness, or no interest in life. Slow down and ask why—*Why am I doing this?* Life has seasons of busyness, but it is impossible to sustain forever. If we don't rein it in on our own terms, life has a way of doing it for us.

- **We rob others of their responsibilities.** When we build dependence on us, it removes the chance for others to learn. *Our doing everything actually hurts more than it helps in the long run.*

- **We teach our daughters to focus on the wrong things.** We unconsciously send our daughters the message that they have to do it all, thus starting a new generation of a never-ending cycle. The good news is that *we can stop the cycle.*

- **We teach our sons never to be truly independent.** Is it possible we have a hand in creating their expectation for women to do it all in the future—personally and professionally? As one mom said, "My son is getting married in a few days and still expects someone else to iron his military uniform—sigh."

Could we entertain the possibility that we are actually removing opportunities for men to fulfill their greatest potential?

LIFE IN THE GREEN ZONE

"Here is what I am willing to do."

This is the kind of language you will hear when in the green zone with Ranee:

- "I will be glad to do *X*; however, let's discuss the priorities … "

- "My schedule does not allow for *X*, but it does allow for *Y*."

- "The best way I can be of help is to do … "

- "Thank you for thinking of me, but my schedule does not permit this right now."

- "I look forward to being able to help in the future."

This is the energy—radiating from the inside out—behind Ranee in the green zone:

- Empowered
- Strong
- Clarity
- Peaceful
- Victorious
- Respected

A key mindset driving many women to dance with the red zone of Ranee is the growing trend to make children the center of the universe. We forget we are raising adults—who are temporarily children. The growing obsession to overdo for children does not serve anyone—the kids, ourselves, or society. Have an honest conversation with yourself, and ask if your well-being is held hostage by the red zones of Kari AND Ranee. You have the power to choose a different reality.

THE REST OF THE STORY: A FOLLOW-UP CONVERSATION WITH RANEE

What was it like to realize your biggest obstacle was an internal mindset?

It was a big eye-opener. I struggle with wanting to say yes to everyone for everything.

Part of your journey has been making time to invest in *you*. That investment has translated into your professional success. Was it worth it?

Absolutely. I have rewired the way I think about many things. Once I became a mom—a working mom—I found it hard to prioritize self-care. It was impossible to do something as simple as get my hair blown out when I was making sure a diaper blowout wasn't on me when I left for work! I always had this belief that my body and appearance were simply a holder for my mind. I didn't realize that my outer polish affected my ability to influence others. While I am not one who will ever be fashion forward, I did outsource the help I needed in this area. I found a service that rents beautiful professional clothing and one that rents jewelry. I didn't have to think about it. Now, I always look put together, and it doesn't break the bank. I also cut my hair and made the look more professional. I was amazed at how much more influence I had once I looked the part of a trusted leader. By investing in myself on multiple levels, I finally earned the promotion I wanted. I increased my salary package by over 30 percent, which says a lot, considering I was already in the top tier. Small actions really do have big impact.

Considering all that you have learned on your journey, what advice would you pass on to other women?

First, consciously choose to underreact. I find that many of our problems are actually the result of our reaction to situations rather than the actual situations. Second, invest in yourself and your career. Hire people to do the busy work. Use that time to invest in your career, your family, or your own free time. We have 168 hours each week. Even if you work 60 of those hours and sleep 56 hours, that still leaves 64 hours a week you can control. Keep a NOT-TO-DO list ... and don't do the things that don't provide you value. Finally, pick your metrics for how you will measure success. I used to be so upset that I couldn't put my daughter to bed every night. The metric of being home every night was impossible to hit. My favorite part of bedtime is reading books to her. So, I changed the metric. Now my goal is to read my daughter fourteen books per week. If I miss a night, I make it up in the morning or over the weekend.

#theRaneestory #myRanee

RANEE

MEANING OF THE LOGO

The diamond is also a prism and an invitation to see the various facets of life. Think about the colors, the rays. Look into the meaning of the number two. Take the letters and analyze them. Search the meaning of the name. Reflect on how diamonds are formed in the natural world. What nugget of treasure is buried deep for you?

INSPIRATION ON THE JOURNEY TO FREEDOM

AFFIRMATIONS

- I don't "have" to do anything.
- It is no one else's responsibility to take care of me.
- Caring for myself IS caring for others.
- My "yes" is a gift—I will offer it wisely.
- I am enough without the "doing."

SONGS TO MOTIVATE YOU

- *Defying Gravity* from *Wicked,* by Kristin Chenoweth and Idina Menzel
- *No,* by Meghan Trainor
- *Golden,* by Jill Scott
- *You Don't Own Me,* by Lesley Gore[74]

MOVIES AND BOOKS TO ENERGIZE YOU

- *The Devil Wears Prada*
- *Mona Lisa Smile*
- *Norma Rae*[75]

TRUE STORIES TO INSPIRE YOU

- *"Q&A: Melinda Gates," from* CBS Sunday Morning *on YouTube.com.*
- *"'I Don't Need Her Permission': Art as a Weapon for Women" at GreatBigStory.com.*
- *"Liz Jackson: Designing for Inclusivity" at 99u.adobe.com*[76]

HEALING MODALITIES TO ASSIST YOU

- *Ylang Ylang oil, by Young Living—A single oil best applied over the heart region that helps you feel complete.*

- *Add a gram of sea or kosher rock salt to a glass spray bottle and then add distilled water. Mix and let sit for a few minutes, then add fifteen to twenty drops of lavender and five to eight drops of lemon and peppermint. Use as a spray.*

- *Roman chamomile—Calming and sanctifying.*

- *Flower essence: Calendula—Release despair, sorrows, the carrying of too many "cares," and heartaches.*

- *Flower essence: Gladiolas—Strength of present time, awareness, and readiness to give/receive.*

When have you been trapped by Ranee's mindset of "I have to meet all demands"? How does this show up professionally?

_____

_____

_____

_____

_____

_____

Have you ever jumped in to do something like Ranee, only to realize later you had other options?

_____

_____

_____

_____

_____

What are the unintended consequences for others in our world if we keep jumping in to do everything?

_____

_____

_____

_____

_____

_____

THE GABRIELLA STORY

I NEED PERMISSION OR APPROVAL

Gabriella's career was at a turning point. At forty-eight, she was still haunted by the sudden loss of a job years earlier in her career. Despite having been a successful supervisor, when the time came to let someone go, she was the chosen one, even though she was also the only one with the requisite engineering degree. Was it because she was a woman? Was it because she was African American? "No," her employees told her. "It's because you don't play the game. You care too much about us, and the higher-ups don't like it."

The loss devastated her. Six years of her life dedicated to the company, only to have it end with the rug being yanked out from under her. *I did everything they asked me to do,* she believed. *Is learning to play the game the only way I can succeed professionally?* A dark cloud descended over her enthusiasm. That experience planted seeds of doubt, which then led to her second-guessing herself at every turn.

Fast-forward almost a decade. Her career had been like a roller coaster—lots of ups and downs. Occasionally mentors showed up, guiding Gabi when possible. "Build your network," the mentors would remind her. After enduring a tough boss, shedding countless tears, and gaining fifty pounds, Gabi had serious doubts about whether professional success was really worth it. She continued to hold on—by a thread. She now had two young children, and life's priorities were pulling her in different directions. "Walking the fence, I had convinced myself that I would never fit in."

In 2013, Gabi attended a workshop sponsored by the Women's Network, where she was introduced to the concept of *jumping into the driver's seat* of her career. It made total sense, and it was something she could do. So Gabi started making changes, slowly at first. One of those changes was to invest energy in herself again. She wanted to appear polished—an attempt to erase the lingering doubt that still clouded her confidence. She was tired of placing everyone else ahead of her own self-care.

In 2016, Gabi showed up at another women's event where I was one of the speakers. It was in the Building Your Leadership Brand session, where participants learned about mindsets and how to change them. Gabi did not realize it, but she was finally ready to shift an internal mindset that had been holding her back all these years.

After my session, Gabi came up to me. She told me about the internal battle she was fighting when it came to office politics—how paralyzed she felt, and again, asking herself if it was all worth it. "Kim, I don't know if I can do it anymore," she said. "Do you have any advice about how I should handle the politics? I am so tired of not being me." What Gabi didn't verbalize was how the internal battle was draining her spirit. One conversation was all it took to see how tired, worn out, and unmotivated she was. It was obvious that she had so much talent to offer, but she had unknowingly placed herself in a cage, thinking she could not step out. *Why is she waiting for permission?* I wondered. *Why is she acting like a kitten when she has the strength of a lion trapped inside?*

"Gabi, has it ever occurred to you that maybe you don't have to change who you are? That it is quite possible *you* are meant to change *the culture*? Don't allow the environment to define you. You have the power to redefine it," I said.

In that moment, Gabi began to see her career through a different lens. She realized that she did not have to *navigate* politics; she had the power to *change* the politics. "That aha moment was transformational. It was like I was hit over the head," Gabi said. Her newfound confidence propelled her into situations where she was able to demonstrate her unique skill set. On one occasion, she was able to fix a problem because she saw it differently than others, and she saved her company $77 million in the process.

"At the end of the day, I embraced the fact that I was uniquely suited to do what was needed during times of enormous change. I started to focus on gaps in the company and took initiative, despite the fact that I did not fit the mold of what company execs looked like," Gabi said.

When asked about her interest in future positions, Gabi boldly rose to the occasion. "I want executive-level growth," she stated. "I know I probably can't check off the boxes required, but I don't feel like the rules apply to me. I am not being arrogant. I am simply confident that the business model is changing and needs to invest in people like me."

Much to her surprise, the senior leader *agreed*, and things have not been the same since. Gabi has been asked to lead assignments all over the world, and she is on the fast track to the executive level she now realizes she deserves. It is an exciting time, and her confident energy radiates from the inside out.

It has been less than one year since she gave herself permission to shift the way she viewed company politics. Turns out, she didn't need a year. She had the power all along.

| I need permission/ approval | ▶ | I TRUST my own decisions | ▶ | I can move forward *in* confidence |

LIFE WITH GABI IN THE RED ZONE

"I need permission or approval."

This is the kind of language you will hear when in the red zone with Gabi:

- "I'm just trying to do ... "

- "I'm not sure if I can do it."

- "Maybe I am not in the right place."

- "I am so tired of waiting for ... "

- "Won't they ever change?"

This is the energy—often unspoken and unconscious—behind Gabi in the red zone. Circle those that resonate with you:

- Powerless
- Caged in
- Doubtful
- Controlled by others
- Anger or apathy

- Uncertainty
- Not measuring up
- Apologetic
- Vulnerable

LOOKING FARTHER DOWN THE ROAD

Here are some unintended consequences to consider when we spend time with Gabi in the red zone:

- **Powerlessness begins to slip in, but we don't realize it.** We grow weary of yearning for things to be different. We tend to question ourselves, wondering what we are doing wrong. The self-doubt is rooted in Kari's expectation of perfection, the first sister in the Sisterhood of Seven.

- **Resentment grows as time slips by.** The resentment bubbles up in odd places, surprising everyone, including ourselves. Professional unhappiness often spills over into personal life, and vice versa. We feel our energy draining. We wonder why we have lost our zest for life.

- **We teach our daughters to wait.** We teach them to hold back and look for someone else to give them permission to move forward. We unconsciously communicate that's just "the way things are done." Over time, Powerlessness seeps in as our girls wonder why the world seems more challenging each day.

- **We teach our daughters not to trust their own decisions.** We unconsciously send the message that the opinions of others are more important than their own.

- When our sons see us waiting for permission or approval, it becomes the norm. **They eventually become blinded to gender issues.** Is it possible that we set the stage for them to move forward in life *unaware* of the need to consciously value both men *and* women?

LIFE IN THE GREEN ZONE

"I can move forward in confidence."

This is the kind of language you will hear when in the green zone with Gabi:

- "I don't know what I was waiting for."

- "I know deep down what to do."

- "I don't have to search for the answer outside anymore."

- "My confidence is unshakable now."

- "I can't wait for the future to unfold."

This is the energy—radiating from the inside out—behind Gabi in the green zone:

- Freedom
- Bold
- Love of self
- Worthy
- Empowered

- Energized
- Excited
- Possibilities
- Resolute
- Purposeful

THE REST OF THE STORY:
A FOLLOW-UP CONVERSATION WITH GABI

What was it like to realize the biggest thing standing in your way was an internal mindset? Did you even realize you were waiting for permission or approval?

I had no idea I was waiting for permission, but it all makes sense now. Self-doubt had unconsciously become a part of my narrative when I was laid off in the previous role. I had to figure out how to do this job and be me. The self-speak is so crucial to your success. Once I shifted my internal dialogues, things really did start changing for me.

What did it feel like when you started to step into that personal power after your aha moment? What might it look like to someone who is still stuck?

If you're comfortable, then you're stuck. Get challenged to grow in your business, expand your expertise, or expand your impact. Realize what you can do better than anyone else in your business. If you don't have that, get it—get it for yourself. It's not until you realize your value that you walk in it. Be the expert that you seek.

What words of encouragement do you have for your sisters on a similar journey?

The light comes on when you know your worth to the business and to yourself. The light comes on when you make a decision to turn it on. Once the light comes on, each of us can illuminate the darkness. Even when you seem to be losing, it may set you up for your biggest win. Once I understood me and what made me, I started walking in my power. I have not looked back since.

What are some of the biggest lessons you hope to teach your sons about a woman owning her power?

Give yourself grace and the ability to be you, being powerful. My parents are from a generation where it was okay to be the status quo and fit in. I now know that being me is more important than fitting in. I teach my boys to own their power. I tell them they do not have to be like mommy or daddy. Own your strengths and know that your strengths will change over time.

I'm all about legacy right now for my kids and grandkids. I want to have a network that will enable my kids to be powerful and own their strengths when they choose their life path. I'm all about connection, legacy, and abundance. I want to listen to what's not being said when I meet a person and how I can fulfill that unspoken question, desire, or passion they don't know how to vocalize! I want that connection to translate into a life lesson for my lineage that will ultimately result in abundance for them—spiritually, mentally, emotionally, physically, and financially. Ultimately, I want them to be able to move forward in confidence, no matter what happens in life.

#theGabistory #myGabi

GABRIELLA

MEANING OF THE LOGO

The lesson in the fractal of the fern is divine order. A fern does not need permission or approval to do what it knows, to be what it is designed to be. Neither do you. You are naturally designed for a purpose. It is seeded deep within your heart. Much like a flower that does not have to be told how to grow, neither do you. Your responsibility is to provide the needed elements to flourish—sun, water, food—and even that is not a controlled process. Marvel at the design of the fern down to the smallest of leaves. Embrace the wonder of divine order.

INSPIRATION ON THE
JOURNEY TO FREEDOM

AFFIRMATIONS

- I choose to trust my own decisions.
- Owning my power requires no apology.
- I choose to get out of my own way.
- I got this.

SONGS TO MOTIVATE YOU

- *Freedom,* by Beyoncé
- *Confident,* by Demi Lovato

- *What Doesn't Kill You (Stronger),* by Kelly Clarkson

- *Greatest Love of All,* by Whitney Houston

- *Grateful,* by Rita Ora77

MOVIES AND BOOKS TO ENERGIZE YOU

- *Erin Brockovich*

- *Wrinkle in Time* directed by Ava DuVernay

- *G.I. Jane*[78]

TRUE STORIES TO INSPIRE YOU

- *"Nigeria's First Female Car Mechanic Is Changing the World"* at GreatBigStory.com.

- *"A Saudi Woman Who Dared to Drive,"* by Manal al-Sharif at Ted.com.

- *"The Septuagenarian Fighting Hate with a Spray Can,"* by Atika Shubert and Nadine Schmidt on CNN.[79]

HEALING MODALITIES TO ASSIST YOU

- *Valor oil, by Young Living—A blend that promotes feelings of confidence and courage. Can be applied to wrists or on feet, also works well when diffused.*

- *Frankincense—Supports balances and uplifts emotions. Helps maintain healthy cell functions.*

- *Flower essence: Iris—Access dreamtime consciousness, explore your imagination, lead with creative flow.*

- *Stones—Moonstone (creates harmony within and strengthens intuition) oil.*

REFLECTION

Gabriella encourages us to think about when we hold ourselves back by seeking permission or approval. How does that show up in your life—personally or professionally?

_____

_____

_____

_____

Why have many women learned not to trust their own decisions? Do you remember if or when you internalized this mindset?

_____

_____

_____

_____

How does moving into the green zone of freedom inspire you to discover the power within and live your fullest life?

_____

_____

_____

_____

THE DARSHA STORY

I SHOULD ACCEPT WHAT IS SAID (OR DONE)

Darsha works for a global company with high expectations for its leaders. Emotional intelligence, agility, and self-discipline are givens. Leaders must have a thirst for excellence, a relentless pursuit of innovation, and an endless reservoir of energy. Darsha had all of that and more.

"My boss said the leadership team did not feel I was ready for a team manager role. I am so frustrated! I moved my family all the way across the country to help launch this site. What else do I have to do to show I am committed to my career?" said Darsha.

Darsha, thirty-four years old and a mother of three, was her family's primary breadwinner. On paper, things looked good: she was working with one of the most recognizable brands in the world. Her company was experiencing lightning growth across multiple industries, creating a blueprint for how to thrive in a digital world. Her Bachelor of Arts in history was an unlikely admission ticket into the wild west of the digital jungle. However, Darsha's expertise in research, sales, and operations support put her on the fast track to success. For five years, she poured her heart and soul into her career, waiting for the right opportunity. Finally, it arrived.

Darsha was invited to take on the intense challenge of launching a new site halfway across the country. After much thought and convincing—*It will lead to advancement soon,* she promised her husband—she made the difficult decision to relocate her entire family. With high hopes for a bright future, they left all family ties behind and headed west.

Months passed with no word of advancement—not even a whisper. No matter how hard she worked, Darsha was beginning to wonder if she would ever move up that ladder. It seemed like no matter what she did, it was never enough for her boss and the leadership team. *Did I move my family across country for something that was never going to happen? Did I take a lateral career change for nothing?* Darsha wondered.

She believed there would be tremendous career growth for those who got in early at this new site in her new home state. However, all her attempts to discuss applying for higher-level positions were met with, "You're not ready," or, "We don't think you're operating on that level yet."

These frustrations were still fresh in her mind when she attended a company-sponsored International Women's Conference in April 2017. While attending a breakout session focused on mindsets that hold women back in leadership, Darsha heard a statement that changed her life. "One of the mindsets was, *I should accept what is said*," she said, marveling. "That statement hit me like a two-by-four over the head. Yes, I did walk into that conference feeling powerless—like a victim. But I left with renewed determination to rewrite my narrative."

Darsha started this rewrite by approaching her advancement much more strategically. She gathered the statistics that would speak to the impact she had on the new site. She requested new meetings with her boss and members of the leadership team. In essence, she took ownership of crafting her professional narrative: one focused on all the skills she brought to the table and all that she had accomplished beyond the short year she'd been at the site.

"Darsha, I had no idea you had this much experience. Why didn't you tell us before now?" asked her boss. While the position she originally wanted had been given to another person, a project opportunity came up unexpectedly. This quasiadvancement provided an opportunity to showcase her skills. She was able to prove that she was ready for the promotion she had been seeking all along.

Four short months after the women's conference, Darsha's boss called her into his office. He shared the good news: she received the promotion. "You might want to sit down before you open that offer envelope," he said.

"I could not believe my eyes," Darsha said. "It was a 66 percent increase over what I was making before. I can't tell you how life changing this was for my family. I guess moving across the country paid off. And to think, I could have missed it if I had simply accepted what was said."

Her sisters nod in agreement. "Amazing what can happen when you discover the power within and live your fullest life."

| I should accept what is said | ▸ | I CAN pause, reflect and choose | ▸ | I choose to rewrite the narrative |

LIFE WITH DARSHA IN THE RED ZONE

"I should accept what is said (or done)."

This is the kind of language you will hear when in the red zone with Darsha:

- "Well, okay, I guess so."

- "I guess I should just accept what my boss said."

- "I am beginning to wonder if things will ever change."

- "Am I the only one who feels this way? Ugh!"

- "Why do *they* do or say that? Ugh!"

This is the energy—often unspoken and unconscious—behind Darsha in the red zone. Circle those that resonate with you:

- Powerless
- Lack of belief in self
- Enslaved
- Trapped
- Tired
- Resentful
- Doubtful of one's ability

- Hopeless
- Confined
- Misunderstood
- Longing for freedom
- Apathetic
- Resigned

The foundation of the #MeToo movement is rooted in the red zone of Darsha. In the United States, we have the propensity to take things to the extreme. It is part of our charm ... and our nemesis. The #MeToo movement now has as many against it as for it—men and women alike. Let's take a moment to rise above the chaos. The movement is symbolic of a larger story still unfolding. It is a red flag alerting us to the pervasive disrespect that is baked into our systems. At its core, it is a blatant disregard for human dignity. This disre-

spect is slowly morphing to impact our sons as well. Think pedophilia. Think hazing deaths. These issues are two sides of the same coin.

May we also consider the significance of how #MeToo goes far beyond the United States. In many countries, the basic rights for women we take for granted are nonexistent. In 2017, the #MeToo movement spread to eighty-five countries, bringing light to a very dark subject. When considering the movement within the context of a #globalsisterhood, is it possible that the US is serving as a point of light? As a catalyst for change? Perhaps the movement is asking us to consider the bigger picture. Rarely is an issue what it appears to be at first glance.

See page 195 for more about what is truly at stake. The interdependence with our global sisters is an important leverage for all.

LOOKING FARTHER DOWN THE ROAD

Here are some unintended consequences to consider when we spend time with Darsha in the red zone:

- **Our success is kept in a holding pattern.** We find ourselves held hostage by the Narrative. We know we have more potential, but we are unsure how to unleash it. We become adept at talking ourselves out of what we really want and settling for much less—personally and/ or professionally.

- **We no longer trust ourselves.** Our gut or intuition sends signals that something isn't right, but we are often paralyzed. Self-doubt takes over. We find ourselves confined by the "everyone else believes it" bias. We lose touch with the intuitive intelligence we are born with.

- **Our daughters watch us accept when others place us in a box.** They wonder, *Are we supposed to do the same?* This leads to teaching our daughters to follow the rules, no matter what. To be a good girl. Our daughters learn to be hesitant to push back. This rule-following mentality affects the rest of their lives, especially in the professional world, where taking risks is rewarded.

- **We are unconsciously trapped by the Narrative.** We model for our sons the type of responses they should expect from women, personally and professionally. We actually perpetuate the cycle of "this is the way things are done," ultimately becoming a partner in keeping the Narrative alive—often unknowingly.

LIFE IN THE GREEN ZONE

"I choose to rewrite the narrative."

This is the kind of language you will hear when in the green zone with Darsha:

- "I have the power to change this."

- "Here is what I am going to do. I am not waiting on *X* any longer."

- "Well, let's see about that."

- "I am not waiting for someone else to do *X* anymore."

- "It feels like the wool is gone from my eyes—wow."

This is the energy—radiating from the inside out—behind Darsha in the green zone:

- Empowered
- Hopeful
- Brave
- Proud
- Growth
- High frequency
- Freedom of expression
- Respected

- Joyful
- Abundance
- Fueled and charged
- Enlightened
- Expansive
- Complete
- Renewed energy

THE REST OF THE STORY: A FOLLOW-UP CONVERSATION WITH DARSHA

Can you describe the aha moment at the conference when you realized Darsha resonated with you?

My aha moment came when we broke into small groups at the conference. We were asked to have different conversations based on the red, yellow, and green mindsets of the sisters so we could see the self-fulfilling prophecy in action.[80] *Our table happened to have Darsha as the sister we were describing. Right before the exercise started, I had been talking with the table about my frustration with my manager and my career. I had ended my sentence with, "Well, I guess I just need to accept what they're telling me." When we were assigned Darsha, everyone at the table gasped and said, "Oh my gosh—it's you!" They had me lead the discussion on how I felt currently and then had me walk through the steps to rewrite my own narrative. It was powerful!*

Let us be reminded of the power of a self-fulfilling prophecy. Most people believe the problem is "out there"—that if the other person would change, then everything would be okay. The self-fulfilling prophecy, however, shows otherwise. The power is with OUR beliefs and assumptions.

What was that session like to realize perhaps the thing standing in your way was an internal mindset?

I felt completely blown away as I started thinking about this differently. Once I questioned why I was simply accepting what I was told, I finally saw the path clearly. I felt energized, and it lit a fire inside of me to go after what I wanted. As women, we're taught to be assertive, not aggressive. I felt like I had been assertive, but I still wasn't getting anywhere. So it really made me feel empowered that I could be more intentional with what I wanted. I had the power to explain what I had accomplished in my career—using impact numbers—and revisit the promotion opportunity with my boss. I had assumed he knew all of my skills. It ended up that he had no idea of all the things I had done before I started working with him. That was a big lesson for me! The experience taught me that it's okay to look at things differently and not to be afraid to push back.

What did it feel like when you started to step into that personal power? What might it look like to someone who might still be stuck?

I felt powerful and hopeful. When I was stuck, I was spending a lot of time blaming others: "How can they not see all that I've done?!" "I'm already doing X, Y, and Z; what more do they need me to do to show I'm ready?!"

If you are trying to advance your career and find yourself uttering phrases that sound powerless, like I did, it's time to take a hard look at yourself. Ask yourself, "What have I shown my manager about this, this, and this project? Does my manager know I implemented this process change and it resulted in our metrics exceeding targets by X amount?"

It is important to remember that no one is a mind reader. Simply because they are your manager/boss doesn't mean they know everything you've done. It's important to be an advocate for yourself and be your own cheerleader, like Jalila's green zone.

You have been inspired to share your excitement with other women so they can change their lives too. What do you want to share with our sisters?

So often, women internalize the message they are to be seen and not heard. Unfortunately, this really filters into our careers. For me, it's about encouraging women to be more vocal about what they want—that being seen as intentional in your goals isn't a bad thing. I've become so passionate about developing women's careers that I've started a women's chapter at my site. Our main focus is career development. I'm already starting to see an impact on other women. I've helped with resume reviews, interview prep, and career development planning. It's great to see so many women get excited about their careers.

#theDarshastory #myDarsha

DARSHA

MEANING OF THE LOGO

Darsha speaks of wisdom, to have vision. The belief that "I should accept what is said" blinds you to the creation that is embedded within your heart. You know when things are not right, so why cave in? The world is in much need of each of you to assess what is believed and reimagine it. Every new creation or belief was established because someone decided it a long time ago. You are as powerful as they. The other connection with Darsha's logo is that eyes are the gateway to the soul. Eyes are the gateway to compassion for yourselves and for others. Love softens the gaze in which we "see."

INSPIRATION ON THE
JOURNEY TO FREEDOM

AFFIRMATIONS

- I am writing my life story—day by day, decision by decision.

- Change my words, change my world.

- I no longer fear the unknown; I courageously embrace it.

- My courage will open doors—for me and others.

SONGS TO MOTIVATE YOU

- *Fighter,* by Christina Aguilera

- *Feeling Good,* by Nina Simone

- *Speechless,* by Naomi Scott in *Aladdin*

- *Roar,* by Katy Perry

- *Own It,* by The Black Eyed Peas[81]

MOVIES AND BOOKS TO ENERGIZE YOU

- *Hidden Figures,* by Margot Lee Shetterly

- *The Help,* by Kathryn Stockett

- *Untamed,* by Glennon Doyle[82]

- *Hope for the Flowers,* by Trina Paulus

- *A Politics of Love,* by Marianne Williamson[83]

- *What Is a Girl Worth?: My Story of Breaking the Silence and Exposing the Truth about Larry Nassar and USA Gymnastics,* by Rachael Denhollander[84]

TRUE STORIES TO INSPIRE YOU

- *"Creating Community with Spain's All-Female Cricket Team" at GreatBigStory.com.*

- *"Bodybuilding at 80" at GreatBigStory.com.*

- *"Brave And Tragic: A Story Of Being One Of The Mengele Twins In The Holocaust" on Facebook.com.*

- *"How a News Anchor Broke the Mold and Found Her Voice" at GreatBigStory.com.*

- *"Blowing Up Stereotypes with a Chemistry Professor" at GreatBigStory.com.*[85]

HEALING MODALITIES TO ASSIST YOU

- *Lavender—Promotes consciousness and peace, as well as emotional well-being. Allows the feeling of "openness."*

- *Copaiba—Calms and supports the nervous system, heart, and respiratory system.*

- *Cassia—Supports digestions of processes, supports healthy immune system and response systems.*

- *Marjoram—Supports a healthy nervous system and cardio-vascular system.*

REFLECTION

When have you been trapped by Darsha's mindset of "I should accept what is said (or done)"? How does this show up professionally?

_____

_____

_____

_____

How is the #MeToo movement tied to Darsha's mindset? Where else in society have women acquiesced to accepting the status quo?

_____

_____

_____

_____

Does the meaning of the logo resonate with you? What else would you add?

_____

_____

_____

_____

THE AVALENE STORY

The solidly confident, graciously proud Avalene of today is quite different from the quiet, accommodating Avalene of the past. To fully appreciate how close she came to taking the path of least resistance, let us wind back the clock.

Growing up in a small town steeped in middle-class values, Avalene quickly learned that hard work and perseverance were the recipes for success. She worked her way through school and graduated with a bachelor's degree in business. Her first job led her down the path of IT, an ideal fit for her natural troubleshooting mind and problem-solving skills. She liked to think of herself as a modern-day Indiana Jones, searching for hidden treasures in a jungle of code. Steady, measured success was the linear formula she was taught. Move from point A to point B and then to point C. *Don't get too far ahead of yourself* and *first, pay your dues* were the philosophies she internalized. Stability was the holy grail. Sure, at times she sensed an internal battle within herself because she also wanted room to grow. Stability *and* growth—were they mutually exclusive, or could you have both? Avalene wasn't sure of the answer, and she wasn't sure she was willing to risk finding out.

Her first job was good; however, due to an unstable economy, the company closed. *This time I'll pick a better field,* she told herself: the solid stable of academia. So, she moved several hours away to pursue an IT position with a legendary university. Yes, she was completely overqualified for the job, but Avalene was determined to do whatever it took to land in a place she could professionally call home. Even if that meant underselling herself. *Just for now,* she rationalized.

With a foot in the door, she settled in quickly, and that was that ... or so she thought. A year passed. Avalene's internal desire to grow demanded more and more attention, but controlled by the status quo mentality—you do things the proper, expected way—she continued to dismiss those growth impulses, although it was taking more and more conscious effort to do so.

Each week, she would look over her company's internal job postings, dismissing most opportunities as out of her league and passing over others because she did not have the preferred requirements. One week, however, one posting stopped her in her tracks. She read it over several times, each time talking herself out of the opportunity. The position required a lot of interaction with VPs and senior leaders. The sheer thought of interacting with executives at that level intimidated her. *I am still new in my field,* she told herself. *It is too much of a stretch for me.* More negative self-talk beat her down—*I should be grateful for the job I have already. I'm not sure I can do this*—and she talked herself right out of applying for the position.

Two months later, Avalene came face to face with what was holding her back from the growth she so desired. She was reading an article about how men and women approach the job application process differently. One sentence felt strangely familiar: "Women apply for jobs only when they have 100% of the qualifications, yet men apply when they have only 60% of the qualifications." *Why is that?* she wondered. *Don't they think they're qualified enough?* And then it hit her. That mindset—*I am not qualified enough*—was her internal battle.

Once she realized exactly what was holding her back—a mindset—she knew it was time to change the way she thought. She finished reading the article and returned to work the following day with a renewed commitment to find the confidence to go after this stretch assignment. For three long months, she went through the interview process. Avalene studied and prepped harder than she ever had for a position. "I knew I had to get their attention, so I did a lot of homework."

It was a Thursday afternoon. Avalene's phone rang, and she saw it was the interviewer. *This is it,* she thought. Taking a deep breath, she picked up the phone. "We appreciated all of your effort—it was noted by everyone on the committee.

But we have decided to go with someone who has more experience," he stated. After expressing her appreciation for the opportunity, Avalene asked sincerely, "What can I do differently next time?"

What was supposed to be a short five-minute talk turned into a fifteen-minute conversation. Avalene hung up, disappointed but proud of herself for trying.

On Friday morning, the phone rang, and she noticed it was the interviewer again. "I have thought about this all night and have revisited our decision about the position," he began. "Even though you don't have all the experience, I really do feel you are the right one for the position. Will you consider our offer to hire you?" Surprised and elated, Avalene answered with an enthusiastic "Yes!" and took a giant step into her new future.

LIFE WITH AVALENE IN THE RED ZONE

"I'm not qualified enough."

This is the kind of language you will hear when in the red zone with Avalene:

- "I should be grateful for the job I have already."

- "I'm not sure I can do this."

- "I am loyal to *X* right now—there will be another opportunity later."

- "Should I or shouldn't I?"—signs of an internal battle.

- "I am not sure if I am ready for that yet."

This is the energy—often unspoken and unconscious—behind Avalene in the red zone. Circle those that resonate with you:

- Lacking confidence or minimal confidence
- Whispering
- Wandering
- When is my turn?
- Distrusting of the future
- Jealousy
- Lacking

- Fearful
- Doubtful
- Pained
- Striving
- Petty
- Strife
- Unsure
- Uncomfortable

LOOKING FARTHER DOWN THE ROAD

Here are some unintended consequences to consider when we spend time with Avalene in the red zone:

- **Opportunities slip through our fingers.** All of our actions are interdependent. When we rise, our sisters rise. This is a privilege of sisterhood, not a burden. Because we often love our sisters enough—often more than ourselves—this can give us courage.

- **We become paralyzed by our internal battles.** We unconsciously shift into a waiting mentality and grow restless. We start to feel unsettled, even unappreciated. We begin to wonder if we are in the right place. We wonder if we will ever have the confidence to move on. We are unaware that we have placed ourselves in a box, and we forget that we have the power to climb out.

- **Unknowingly, we send our daughters a message of low confidence.** We plant seeds of doubt: *If mom can't do it, how can I?* We teach our daughters to wait for opportunities instead of creating them. We perpetuate the myth that the formula for success *lies in someone else's hands*—not our own. The seeds of doubt plow fertile ground for the red zone of Nikki to take root (I'm okay in the background).

- **Sons can become trapped by believing they have to *save* mom.** When a mother believes she's not qualified and shifts into a mindset of Powerlessness, her son can step in as the protector. Seeds of doubt are often planted in these sons' minds about the ability of women in general. As a result, some of these young boys grow into men who exert control over women, personally or professionally, due to this unconscious belief. We each have the power to stop this cycle.

LIFE IN THE GREEN ZONE

"There is enough for me AND you."

This is the kind of language you will hear when in the green zone with Avalene:

- "I can do this!"

- "I can learn anything I set my mind to."

- "I feel like a success story—wow!"

- "I look for opportunities to encourage other women now."

- "I can't help but share with women that there is another way!"

This is the energy—radiating from the inside out—behind Avalene in the green zone:

- Brave
- Proud
- Adventurous
- Daring
- Dreaming
- Self-assured
- Validated
- Hopeful

- Creative
- Solid
- Bold
- Gracious
- Energized
- Determined

THERE IS ENOUGH FOR ME AND YOU

Celebrating the success of another does not diminish our own. Celebrating the beauty of another does not diminish our own. The power lies in focusing on abundance. With each individual success, it is a building block for the sisterhood collectively. Embrace the idea that your success is my success and my success is your success.

#sweetsisters #globalsisterhood

THE REST OF THE STORY: A FOLLOW-UP CONVERSATION WITH AVALENE

How did you feel about life before you decided to go after your dream job?

There was an internal battle going on inside my head. After all, I had been with the university just under a year. Who was I to think I could move on? Didn't I need to be loyal to the person who hired me in the first place? I could not see past the many roadblocks I placed in the way. Oddly enough, most of the roadblocks I imagined didn't even exist. We often make things harder than they have to be. I was very fragile going into the conversation with my boss at the time. Surprisingly, she was very encouraging. What a relief! She inspired me to do the same for others from this point forward.

What was it like to realize perhaps the biggest thing standing in your way was an internal mindset?

It was so freeing to let go of the self-doubt. Persistence and determination have always been a part of my career plan, but my internal doubts were burdensome. Learning how my mindset was holding me back opened my eyes; it was educational and motivational. The time span between becoming aware of my mindset and my shift to do something about it was very short. It was like the light turned on in my head. I'm really not sure I would have applied for my dream job had I not gained this awareness. I might still be in the red zone today waiting for "my turn."

Any words of wisdom to encourage other women?

If you want something, don't talk yourself out of it. Surprisingly, other women began to reach out to me while I was going through the three-month interview process. They kept asking, "What did you do to move yourself forward?" I shared that I had to get out of my own way! I also gave way too much power to the "preferred master's degree" qualification. Don't allow yourself to get stuck on the preferred qualifications. Instead, focus on the value you bring to the table. You get an entirely different outcome when you shift your focus. I love my job now, and it has exceeded my expectations. This position bumped me to a 64 percent increase once I included my benefits. I want other women to experience the same success!

#theAvalenestory #myAvalene

AVALENE

MEANING OF THE LOGO

There is much magic in the life of a butterfly. It offers a glimpse into transformation. Ask yourself how it parallels your life. The journey of a butterfly is faith. It has to have faith to go dormant and be in the cocoon for a period of rest. But rest is not really what is happening. It is more like *space*, allowing for a new beautiful being to emerge. Why walk on so many legs using much effort to cover distances like a caterpillar when you were designed to fly? Allow yourself to marvel at the colors, the variations, the designs—it will invite you to a new way to view yourself and others. Childlike wonder is the energy of the butterfly. Stillness, softness, yet strength to have made it through the transformation. The logo offers the cycle of birth and life. While it lives, it brings much joy. Is your life bringing joy to the world?

INSPIRATION ON THE
JOURNEY TO FREEDOM

AFFIRMATIONS

- I have an innate ability to learn and grow.

- Fear has no place in my world.

- I am already a success—the rest of the world will catch up soon.

- I choose to be brave.

- My footsteps will lead others down a brave path someday.

SONGS TO MOTIVATE YOU

- *Salute,* by Little Mix

- *I'm Coming Out,* by Diana Ross

- *I'm Every Woman,* by Whitney Houston

- *You Will (The Own Song),* by Jennifer Hudson and Jennifer Nettles[86]

MOVIES AND BOOKS TO ENERGIZE YOU

- *Mean Girls*

- *The Secret Life of Bees,* by Sue Monk Kidd

- *A League of Their Own*[87]

TRUE STORIES TO INSPIRE YOU

- *"Inside Japan's Only All-Female Sushi House" at GreatBig-Story.com.*

- *"Upstanders: A Racist's Rehabilitation" by Howard Schultz and Rajiv Chandrasekaran at Stories.Starbucks.com.*

- *"Instigators: The Midwife of La Cienega Boulevard" at GreatBigStory.com.*[88]

HEALING MODALITIES TO ASSIST YOU

- *Idaho balsam fir or Idaho blue spruce—Brings about feelings of empowerment.*

- *Cassia—Supports digestions of processes, supports healthy immune system and response systems.*

- *Cedarwood—Relaxing and clarifying.*

- *Copaiba—Calms and supports the nervous system, heart, and respiratory system.*

- *Magnolia—Can reduce feelings of anxiety.*

- *Flower essence: Shasta daisy—Unity; we are all petals of the same flower.*

- *Stones—Obsidian (strength and protection).*

REFLECTION

Avalene's green mindset reminds us that we are in this together. Why do women forget this sometimes, and how can we do a better job of supporting each other? What part of the struggle and desire to compete was passed down to us?

_____

_____

_____

_____

Did the logo's meaning of transformation resonate with you? Are you ready to fly?

_____

_____

_____

_____

Any thoughts about how the Narrative has shown up in your world lately? Awareness is the most important part of the journey.

_____

_____

_____

_____

THE JALILA STORY

IF I WORK HARD ENOUGH,
I WILL BE REWARDED

T he unexpected call came late one Friday afternoon. "I am so frustrated right now, Kim; I don't know what to do. Over the years, I've hired you to help many other leaders at this company. Now, I'm calling about me," said Jalila, a leader with whom I had worked for well over a decade. "I just found out I didn't receive the pay increase I'd been promised. *For the third year in a row!* Can you please, please help me see what I am missing?"

Always on the go, Jalila had major responsibilities at a luxury brand experiencing double-digit growth. She had already invested fourteen years in the company, growing its professional development division. Well respected and known for making things happen, Jalila was able to accomplish more than most others. Her drive, expertise, and quest for excellence made her essential to the North American site.

However, Jalila was so focused on *doing* the job that she missed the signs as the company slowly boxed her into exactly where they needed her to be. It took the third time of not being recognized for her to make that call to me. Literally and figuratively, she had reached the end of her rope.

What else did she have to do to be recognized? Her frustration was driven by many unspoken and unanswered questions.

The good news was that this crisis stopped Jalila in her tracks long enough to invest much-needed time into herself. She had fallen into the trap of thinking, *If I work hard enough, I will be rewarded.* The strategy had worked for many years early in her career. However, her professional life "grew up" and reached a predictable point where hard work alone was no longer enough. "When is the last time you invested in your success—your leadership brand, Jalila?" I asked.

"Invest in myself?" She laughed out loud. "Who has time for that? I have work to do!"

For more than ten minutes, she adamantly explained *all* the responsibilities she had, *all* the tasks she had completed, and the growing pressure of *all* the expectations now squarely placed upon her shoulders. "Don't you realize this is the *third* boss I have had in five years? While those leaders are coming and going, I am the one left running this place. There has been no time to invest in me."

The rest of our conversation was uncomfortable. Jalila listened as I explained that the very mindsets that had made her successful up to this point were not enough to take her to the next level. "It's time to focus on increasing your visibility instead of simply working hard," I said. Hesitantly, she considered the possibility that it *was* time to think differently. Not completely convinced but willing to try, she agreed to spend the next three months investing in herself.

"This is not going to be easy. I don't like talking about myself. I am not sure this is really the problem. If the bosses would just do their job ... " she muttered.

"Time will tell," I calmly replied.

Over the next three months, Jalila begrudgingly worked to raise her visibility. With each small step, she started to see things change. Leaders would spend more time with her once she arranged a meeting asking for their insight. Each action was a stepping stone to a new path. Even when she saw progress, she was quick to revert back to, *Do these things really matter? I just want to do my job.* She was not one to waste money, but if the company was investing in having me as her coach, she was going to use the advice. The day arrived when she called about a retreat she was facilitating for upper management. She reached out requesting ideas about how to do it well.

"Now that you have the mechanics planned out, what are you going to do to invest in *your* leadership brand while you are there?" I asked. "How can you use this opportunity as a way to authentically raise your visibility?"

Jalila sighed loudly. "I had not thought of that. Do I really need to? After all, they are there for the retreat, not to listen to me," she hastily explained.

"It is exactly that mindset that led to you not receiving a well-deserved increase for the third year in a row," I reminded her. Silence.

A few moments later, she begrudgingly signed on to my suggestion. "Fine. So how do I do it in a low-key way?"

Strategy in place, her low-key effort worked. Every time she experienced a small success, her confidence grew. Each time her confidence grew, leaders responded positively. Jalila started to believe small actions could have a big impact.

During this process, we stumbled upon a key leverage, which was glaringly obvious once Jalila thought about it. It was so obvious she had missed it for the last three years. It was the promotion process: each year, the bosses would gather in a room to discuss the list of employees who were in line for an increase. Only a certain number of increases was allowed each year—and those limited increases went to the people whose leaders were able to speak the loudest, influence the most, or offer the most compelling case for why their employee was so deserving.

"Jalila, what have you done to prepare your new boss to be able to fight on your behalf when this process starts again?" I asked.

"Nothing. I have done nothing because I assume that, as the boss, they know what to do," Jalila said.

"How can your new boss know what to say on your behalf when you can't even describe to me the value you bring? You are so valuable to the division that many would have difficulty clearly articulating what you do, much less do it in a compelling way." It was becoming clear to us both that perhaps one of the reasons her bosses kept changing—being promoted—was *because* of her hard work. One look at Jalila, and I saw the light bulb come on. And from that moment on, everything shifted.

Less than ninety days later, I received another very different phone call. "Amazing news—I received the pay grade increase this time!" *You go, Jalila,* I thought. *Don't stop now.*

Luckily, she didn't. Eighteen months later, Jalila finally busted out of the box that she unknowingly allowed the company to place her in. She was promoted to a new division with fresh responsibilities. This is what happens when a talented woman finally begins to own and articulate her value.[89]

| If I work hard enough, I will be rewarded | ▶ | I can advocate and CARE for myself | ▶ | I own and articulate my value |

LIFE WITH JALILA IN THE RED ZONE

"If I work hard enough, I will be rewarded."

This is the kind of language you will hear when in the red zone with Jalila:

- "I'm just trying to do my job."

- "Can't talk right now. I am on deadline" (every time you talk to her).

- "I don't have time to do things for myself. Do you know how much I have on my plate?"

- "I will take care of it. I always do."

- "No one around here seems to realize how hard I work."

This is the energy—often unspoken and unconscious—behind Jalila in the red zone. Circle those that resonate with you:

- Busyness (which can blind you to the root cause)
- Heavy
- Burdened
- Doubtful
- Questioning

- Distrustful
- Waiting
- Resentful
- Tired
- Victimhood
- Bitter

LOOKING FARTHER DOWN THE ROAD

Here are some unintended consequences to consider when we spend time with Jalila in the red zone:

- **We train everyone around us to expect it.** Unknowingly, our behavior trains others to allow a disproportionate amount of work to be placed on our laps. They watch as we work ourselves to exhaustion. It is predictable that eventually we will reach a point where we are tired of it! Only we don't realize that we did it to ourselves.

- **We lose sight of the bigger picture.** With our heads down, doing the work becomes the short-term focus as we move from one event to the next. Teaching our children—or others—dependence on us today does not create fertile ground for independence in the future.

- **We pass on a lack of self-care.** Somehow, we have missed the pearl of wisdom that caring for ourselves *is* caring for others. Caring for ourselves is an inside job *first*. As within, so without. The root of the issue is self-respect. We will never receive what we are not willing to give to ourselves.

- **We turn away help unnecessarily.** When others offer help, we often turn it away under the misguided notion that we have to work harder. We can learn to say yes. After all, care has a hidden message for us:

Cherish and

Accept

Respect and support

Every time it is offered!

LIFE IN THE GREEN ZONE

"I own and articulate my value."

This is the kind of language you will hear when in the green zone with Jalila:

- "Owning my value gets easier and easier."

- "I don't wait for anyone else anymore."

- "I definitely feel more confident."

- "I take more risks—you never know what might happen."

- "I feel so much happier and free now."

This is the energy—radiating from the inside out—behind Jalila in the green zone:

- Understood
- Complete
- Tall
- Bold
- Self-full
- Clarity of thought and purpose
- Confident
- Still
- Alive and vibrant
- Tower of strength
- Unshakable
- Strong foundation

TO ALL THE JALILAS

When we are dancing with Jalila, busyness becomes a major blind spot.[90] It is not easy to connect the dots because investing in ourselves is not considered an important item on our to-do list. This is a key characteristic found every single time Jalila's red zone shows up.

THE REST OF THE STORY: A FOLLOW-UP CONVERSATION WITH JALILA

How did it feel to go through the process of learning to advocate for yourself? You went into that process kicking and screaming.

Ha ha, yes, that sounds quite familiar. When we started the coaching process, I felt taken advantage of and under-appreciated. I had invested a lot of my life in making the company successful. I was tired and not sure if it was even possible for me to work any harder. I did not want to leave, but I did wonder if that was going to be the only way I could advance.

As for what changed, I simply started feeling more confident about myself through the process. I started working at a higher level and exposing myself to senior managers. I started taking more risks, which led to more successes. Putting myself out there made a big difference. By the time this current position opened up, I went for it! You know, now that I think about it, maybe it did result from my thinking differently. (Doesn't that sound like the self-fulfilling prophecy in action?)

What does it feel like today, now that you've shifted your perspective and become more comfortable acknowledging your value?

> *I finally learned to see through the bias. Others were resistant to my taking on this new position. I realized they were looking out for themselves, that they had their own interest at heart, not mine. I reached a point where I was confident enough to say to myself, I don't care. I needed to do what is best for me. It was time to grow and change. I stopped trying to please everyone else.*

Now that you can see more clearly, what advice would you offer to other women in the Sisterhood?

> *First, listen to your gut. Talk to others for their insight, but in the end, you are the one who has to live with your decision. In your heart of hearts, you know what is right for you. Listen to yourself.*

#theJalilastory #myJalila

JALILA

MEANING OF THE LOGO

Every snowflake has a different shape. A collection of snow-flakes has the potential to create a winter wonderland of magic or an avalanche. Such is true with the human spirit. Each snowflake knows its worth. The magic of a single snowflake is not always visible at first glance. It is easy to miss the magic when we are rushing about, irritated with the snow. Keep in mind that snowflakes reflect light. What is your light reflecting? Slow down and see the magic.

INSPIRATION ON THE JOURNEY TO FREEDOM

AFFIRMATIONS

- I choose to own the power I do have.
- It is no one else's job to stand up for me.
- I have the strength to stand up for myself.
- The world will value me when I value myself.
- I have the strength to be my biggest advocate.

SONGS TO MOTIVATE YOU

- *Independent Women Part 1,* by Destiny's Child
- *Respect,* by Aretha Franklin
- *Just Fine,* by Mary J. Blige
- *Not a Pretty Girl,* by Ani DiFranco[91]

MOVIES AND BOOKS TO ENERGIZE YOU

- *Legally Blonde*
- *I Am Malala,* by Malala Yousafzai[92]
- *Girl Decoded,* by Rana el Kaliouby, PhD, & Carol Coleman[93]
- *#GIRLBOSS,* by Sophia Amoruso[94]

TRUE STORIES TO INSPIRE YOU

- *"The First Women's Self Defense Studio in the Middle East" at GreatBigStory.com.*

- *"Claressa: Fighting to Stay on Top" at GreatBigStory.com.*

- *"Breaking Silicon Valley's Glass Ceiling" at GreatBigStory.com.*[95]

HEALING MODALITIES TO ASSIST YOU

- *Release oil, by Young Living—Detoxes body of negative emotions, including anger and resentment. Best practice is to apply a drop over your liver.*

- *Rose—Flower essences or oils. A rose spray is also comforting and uplifting.*

- *Grapefruit to detoxify the stressors of "overdoing to overprove it."*

- *Lemongrass—Detoxifies heat-related inflammation, anger, hot flashes.*

- *Frankincense—Supports balances and uplifts emotions. Helps maintain healthy cell functions.*

- *Flower essence: Lilac—Soul celebrations, enhance intention with a celebratory aspect.*

- *Stones—Aventurine (harmonizes mental, physical, and emotional bodies).*

REFLECTION

Jalila is often blinded by busyness. Can you relate? What does busyness do to your ability to connect the dots and see the big picture?

_____

_____

_____

_____

What is your belief system about the concept of time? Is it possible to rewrite that belief and develop a new relationship with the concept of time?

_____

_____

_____

_____

How comfortable are you in advocating for yourself? Why do women struggle with this? When this issue arises, ask yourself, "Is it the system, or is it me?"

_____

_____

_____

_____

THE NIKKI STORY

I'M OKAY IN THE BACKGROUND

Nikki, a midlevel career executive, was identified as a high-potential employee for one of the world's best-known brands, with hundreds of thousands of staff worldwide. She had moved up in operations, had a knack for complex assignments, and was known for challenging the status quo. Nikki knew that it would probably be another five years before she could go after a senior-level executive position. She was paying her dues and following a rather predictable path laid out before her. She was having some success—she had cracked the six-figure mark—but no matter how hard she worked, things were not moving as quickly as she had hoped.

She knew there had to be a better, faster way to grow her professional success, but how? Maybe her confidence level was holding her back. Maybe it was her presentation skills. Surely there was *something* she could do, right?

In the meantime, she was working on a specific goal: to present to an audience of one hundred people without being nervous. For some reason, she could not find the confidence to do so. Nikki had talent, knowledge, technical skills, and savvy to influence others one on one. However, confidence issues kept tripping her up. That's when she reached out to me.

As I helped her polish her presentation skills, we talked about the bigger picture. "Kim, I want to be in that senior-level position," Nikki said. "I'll do whatever it takes to be ready." With that statement, everything shifted—we went from working on Nikki's presentation to building her leadership brand.

We carefully examined every signal she was sending out in her professional world. One seemingly minor detail we decided to change was her professional headshot. As we reviewed the details of her upcoming photo shoot, I asked Nikki what she planned to wear. "Perhaps you could wear a red jacket," I suggested, thinking the color would look striking against her dark-olive skin.

"No! I cannot do that," she quickly retorted. We went through the rest of our session together in silence. As we wrapped up, I decided to give the topic one more try.

"Nikki, would you consider wearing a red jacket for the shoot?"

She began to frown and reject the idea again, but as she opened her mouth, all that came out was a startled, quiet, "Oh no!" She quickly placed her hand over her mouth, and her eyes grew huge. "I just realized why I can't wear a red jacket. Both my parents are from India. In the town they came from, the bride wears red so that all eyes are on her. I can't wear red because I don't want all eyes on me." Tears began to fall on her cheeks. "How am I going to reach that senior executive level if I'm not comfortable with all eyes being on me?"

The "red-jacket moment"[96] played a pivotal role in Nikki's transformation. It completely shifted her perspective. Nikki continued to give everything she had to her company, investing blood, sweat, and tears, but her company could not, would not, catch up with her growth. Within eighteen months, she was recruited to be a high-level director for a major corporation.

It paid for her to relocate her family, she increased her salary by 51 percent, and, most importantly, she stepped into her power with such momentum, there was—and is—no stopping her.

The last time I heard from Nikki was in the form of a text, sent from the private corporate jet: "I could get used to living like this!"

Here is a key part of the story that even I did not know until she shared it recently.

"And to think, none of this would have happened if I did not fight—and I mean *fight*—for the company to invest in me through executive coaching. I had to ask not once, but twice, before they agreed to it. Where would I be if I had given up?"

Did you hear that? She is the one who asked that the company invest in her. And she did not stop until it happened. What a legacy she is creating for her daughters!

| I'm okay in the background | ▶ | I AM powerful and that's okay | ▶ | My power is MUCH needed in this world |

LIFE WITH NIKKI IN THE RED ZONE

"I'm okay in the background."

This is the kind of language you will hear when in the red zone with Nikki:

- "I don't know why I can't find the confidence."

- "I think it is more important to focus on my team."

- "I don't need to be out front. Really … it's okay."

- "I just want to serve and take care of the others."

This is the energy—often unspoken and unconscious—behind Nikki in the red zone. Circle those that resonate with you:

- Hidden
- Shy
- Uncertain
- Low self-importance
- Trapped
- Frightened
- Timid or doubtful
- Hesitant to shine
- Confined by expectations
- Pinned down
- Rule bound

LOOKING FARTHER DOWN THE ROAD

Here are some unintended consequences to consider when we spend time with Nikki in the red zone:

- **It's all about everyone else.** The red zone of Nikki takes the idea of being selfless to the extreme. The question is why? You deserve as much respect, love, and honor as everyone else.

- **Staying in the background—consciously or not— sometimes hides another issue.** The red zone of Nikki can often mask Kari's expectation for perfection. If deep down we believe the world has deemed us as not measuring up in some way (looks, status, intelligence, etc.), it is quite possible we have learned to hide. It would be helpful to remember Kari's green zone: "I am enough."

- **We unconsciously absorb messages about "our place" in the world.** Is it possible we are teaching our daughters and sons that women should be seen, not heard? For our daughters, this translates into missed opportunities throughout life—from the way we introduce ourselves with impact to how we negotiate salaries. The underlying message shows up in our personal world too.

- **Our relationship with power becomes distorted.** Too often, women unconsciously equate power with control. Far too many of us have experienced the controlling side of others. Even more have dealt with unsafe environments—emotionally and/or physically. The opportunity lies in women reestablishing a new healthy relationship with the essence of power.

LIFE IN THE GREEN ZONE

"My power is much needed in this world."

This is the kind of language you will hear when in the green zone with Nikki:

- "I can do this."

- "I can't believe I waited so long!"

- "There is no holding back now."

- "I feel like a weight has been lifted off my shoulders."

- "Amazing what happens when you step into your power."

This is the energy—radiating from the inside out—behind Nikki in the green zone:

- Propelled
- Full of self-love
- Done with doubt
- Fueled by a greater purpose
- Adventurer
- Clarity of purpose
- Soulful
- Calmly confident
- Nonapologetic
- Poised and purposeful
- Genuine

THE REST OF THE STORY: A FOLLOW-UP CONVERSATION WITH NIKKI

Can you describe the aha moment for you?

The red-jacket moment. It hit on all the subconscious issues. Once we addressed those, I felt the breakthrough. The shackles holding me back were removed.

What was it like to realize your biggest obstacle was an internal mindset?

It was like a veil had been lifted, and I could see clearly. I also knew that since it was internal, I was in control and could change it. It would take time, but it was within my power to change.

What did it feel like to rewire that thought process?

It was exciting and scary at the same time. Knowing I was in charge was great, but it also presented me with closed doors I wasn't sure I wanted to open. I had some self-doubt initially that I had to overcome. I was apprehensive at first, a bit overwhelmed by my power. I had to become comfortable in this new skin. I am still amazed by it, and I don't take a minute of it for granted. I still have to remind myself, and sometimes I falter. Every day I feel stronger.

What did it feel like when you started to step into that personal power? What might it look like to someone who might still be stuck?

It felt like I was taking ownership and accountability, which can be scary because this is new territory. I was stuck in the narrative I had defined for myself, and on some level, it was comfortable there. In that world, I knew the rules. This evolved version of myself was like a trust exercise with myself. I was depending on me to catch it when I took a misstep. When I saw myself going back to my old ways, I would call it out mentally and pivot.

The happiness and shock in your voice when you told me about the 51 percent increase was amazing. You shared your excitement of spreading the message to other women so they could change their lives too. Why is that important?

I have taken three mentees under my wing. With all three of them, I was recommended to them as a mentor. A great feeling and honor. One of the mentees said she was so nervous to meet me because of my title, but she felt completely comfortable talking with me when we met—I was a "real" person. That comment made me laugh because I don't see myself based on my title, but it showed me the lenses other people see me through ... how times have changed.

In light of what you have learned on your journey over the past few years, what is the biggest lesson you hope to teach your two daughters?

Don't let yourself get in the way of your greatness. The only thing stopping them from reaching their goal is themselves. They are each other's best friends and biggest supporters. They MUST always help one another achieve the best version of themselves.

#theNikkistory #myNikki

NIKKI

MEANING OF THE LOGO

Soar higher. See the bigger picture that others close to the ground are blinded to. You have an invitation to do that each time you fly in an airplane. See how different the world looks from up high? Fly above the chaos of the world. Nikki's symbol is an invitation. It is a sign that you are never alone. The feather symbolizes many things—spend time reflecting. Connect to your native roots—much wisdom from your Native American sisters at a soul level. This logo relates to Avalene's journey of flight and Darsha's invitation to have vision. Soaring higher gives us perspective. "Climb higher" is the calling card for humanity.

INSPIRATION ON THE JOURNEY TO FREEDOM

AFFIRMATIONS

- I was not made to stand in the shadows.

- Power is not a bad word.

- This world needs me!

- It's okay for me to shine.

SONGS TO MOTIVATE YOU

- *This Is for My Girls,* by Chloe and Halle, Jadagrace, Janelle Monáe, Kelly Clarkson, Kelly Rowland, Lea Michele, Missy Elliott, and Zendaya

- *Run the World,* by Beyoncé

- *Fight Song,* by Rachel Platten

- *Unwritten,* by Natasha Bedingfield

- *Superwoman*, by Alicia Keys[97]

MOVIES AND BOOKS TO ENERGIZE YOU

- *The Moment of Lift: How Empowering Women Changes the World,* by Melinda Gates

- *Fight Like a Mother: How a Grassroots Movement Took on the Gun Lobby and Why Women Will Change the World,* by Shannon Watts

- *The Time Is Now: A Call to Uncommon Courage,* by Joan Chittister

- *Her Story: A Timeline of Women Who Changed America,* by Charlotte S. Waisman and Jill S. Tietjen[98]

TRUE STORIES TO INSPIRE YOU

- *"A Field Between: Former CIA Operative Risks Life to Promote Peace" at GreatBigStory.com.*

- *"The Greatest Showman: 'This Is Me' with Keala Settle" on YouTube.com.*

- *"Taking Back the Neighborhood with an Army of Moms" at GreatBigStory.com.*

- *"A Cafe Run by Heroes" at GreatBigStory.com.*

- *"The Women Making History in Georgia's Justice System" at GreatBigStory.com.*

- *"Afghanistan Female Journalists Risk Their Lives to Tell the News" at GreatBigStory.com.[99]*

HEALING MODALITIES TO ASSIST YOU

- *Sacred mountain oil—Helps to break free from the fear of speaking out.*

- *Bergamot is a solar plexus grounding oil. Stay clear and grounded.*

- *Roman chamomile—Sanctifying of soul self and body.*

- *Fir and basil, combined—Creates a detoxifying and clarifying aspect for body, mind, and soul.*

- *Cassia—Promotes a sense of well-being, used for thousands of years.*

- *Flower essence: Rose—The highest frequency of the flower kingdom, divine intelligent love, soul love, peace and calm, utmost devotion to love, trust, higher soul loves, pure healing.*

REFLECTION

What did you think of Nikki's red-jacket moment? Have you ever been hesitant to be seen? Do you have your own red-jacket moment?

_____

_____

_____

_____

_____

_____

What does the phrase, "This was a trust exercise with myself," mean to you?

_____

_____

_____

_____

What is one action you will take this week based on what you have read?

_____

_____

_____

_____

HOW THE SISTERS
COME TO LIFE

N ow that you've met each sister, it's time to take a step
back and look at the big picture: the Sisterhood as a
whole.

You can download the inspiration guide detailing all
their mindsets—a one-page Sisterhood you can print and
keep with you—at YourLionInside.com.[100] Use it as inspiration to bring out the best of the Sisterhood in your life.

Remember: this is a continuum, one step at a time.
Small actions have a *big* impact. Simply start with the sister
who resonates with you the most. The rest will fall into place.

Keep coming back until mindsets from the green zone
are rooted in your psyche, until you no longer have to consciously choose the empowering mindsets, until they have
become part of your subconscious.

The Sisterhood is for sharing, so I encourage you to share
these mindsets with any woman you believe could benefit

from discovering her own lion inside. If there is one thing we can all agree on, it's that we can often see in each other what we can't see in ourselves. Download a snapshot[101] at EpicenterofChange.com of the past, present, and future and have a conversation with your mother, grandmother, and others. Be a catalyst for the change you seek.

THE SISTERHOOD SHOWS UP WHEN YOU LEAST EXPECT IT

Gabriella is my girl, the sister I am closest to. I call her Gabi. Of all the sisters, she is the one who stays nearest to me. "*I got your back, girl,*" she says. She has wiped my tears away on many occasions. She has cheered me on when I faced challenges. Even as I was in the final stages of writing this book, Gabi reminded me of what is truly being asked by us all: to see things differently in our professional and *personal* lives. The Sisterhood is not limited to work. It shows up at home too.

I unexpectedly married again four years ago. No one was more surprised than I when "never" came knocking at my door. I was blessed with a man who was able to break through my tough exterior and touch the depths of my heart. Our blended families include my daughter, Heather, and his two daughters, his son, granddaughters, and great-granddaughters. For the first time in my life, I learned what unconditional love really means. It was in this heart space that I blossomed. *I was finally safe.* Peter is much older than me, but he remains young in spirit. It was in this safe zone that my husband helped me dissect the messages many women internalize by showing me *how it happens.* He has endured my requests to view our life like a sitcom. I would carefully request emotion be removed from the situation and to lovingly help me discover how a sister shows up. That would be the case with the appearance of Gabi.

It began with a simple discussion about cars. I have a Jeep Wrangler, and we've shared many laughs over my rebellious choice in cars. It was the first car I ever purchased on my own. Despite deep affection for my adventurous pal, there was one other car that would stop me in my tracks. Every. Single. Time. I would drool as she drove by. I would sigh with longing when I saw her parked. My daughter said it was the one thing I have ever said I actually wanted out loud. My husband discovered this. "We should find a used one," he said. I was in shock! "Are you kidding me?" was my reply. Little did I know, Gabi was along for this ride.

On Monday, the day of the 2017 solar eclipse visible in the United States, my husband heard about a used model for sale. We decided to go for a test drive—and viewed one of the most important celestial events of the century at a car dealership. I had great fun test-driving the car. It was like stepping into a dream. I never had the courage to test it out in the real world. Subconsciously, I had filed it away in the wistful *Someday When I Win the Lottery* mental folder. The model we test-drove had everything we were looking for— price, mileage, and care. Except I was not excited about the color—a rich chocolate brown with a camel interior. Keep in mind, back in my dream world, just *thinking* about this car would bring me to tears. But here I was standing beside one, and there was nothing—no feeling at all. I kept waffling back and forth as I discussed it with my husband. I said I wanted to call my daughter, Heather.

My desire to "phone a friend" sparked an intense discussion right there in the parking lot. "You need to learn to think on your own," he stated with conviction. "Why do you need other people's opinion? Why don't you trust your own opinion?"

Valid point. Something I am working on, check.

He told me that choosing a car is a very personal decision based on taste. Deep down, I was torn. I wanted to like the car, but I felt hesitant about the color. Earlier, he had jokingly asked, "What is it about women and colors of cars—geez?"

Now, I knew *he* liked the color. While I didn't like the color, I could feel myself wanting to please him. I was also paralyzed by the fear of making the wrong decision—again. Can you relate? Deep down, unconsciously, I guess I wanted his approval—even though I was forty-eight years old. *Ugh, Gabi—I thought we made peace with this, sista!* Evidently, Gabi and I had some work to do.

Two days later, I found the car I *loved* at a dealer two hundred miles away. I adored the beautiful deep-blue exterior and the gorgeous creamy interior. It fit the mileage specs, was inexpensive to transport, and had been well cared for. And—it made me cry! I could not wait to show my husband. When he came home, he quickly looked at the website on his phone and casually mentioned that the car was not a color he cared for. Without much thought, it appeared that he had dismissed it, mumbling something about looking at it later, and he left.

I was crushed.

It felt like ice water had been dumped all over me. I was surprised by how I felt in that moment. Powerless. Through my journey with the sisters, I know with absolute certainty that when I feel powerless, it is a trigger to figure out what is not right. "*What is going on, Kimberly?*" I asked myself.

An hour later, Peter called to suggest I look at another used car. I quietly internalized the unspoken message (or so I thought): *Keep looking. The choice you made this morning was not a good one.* By now, I *really* did not like how I was feeling. I was confused. *Why did he dismiss what I wanted? He just told me Monday I need to think for myself. I tried to do that today, and yet I was dismissed. What message do I take away from this now? Is this how these limiting mindsets internalize?*

I had a choice. I could choose to internalize that my opinion does not matter and feel my power erode a bit, or I could address it head on. The outcome would be predictable based on which side of Gabi I chose to dance with.

My beloved came home later in the day. I asked if we could have an objective conversation about the car experience—like we were watching a sitcom. He agreed. I showed him the one-page Sisterhood outline and explained how I was wrestling with Gabi. I felt like the red zone of Gabi was winning. I was taking steps to trust my own opinion, but I was baffled about how the car process was unfolding.

Amused but committed, he processed the entire experience with me—*for the benefit of the book*, he said. He explained his thought process: he questioned the logistics of purchasing a car so far away—if it was worth the effort, what could go wrong—all unspoken. He could now see how I might have perceived his silence as not having confidence in my opinion. I told him how thankful I was to be able to have this conversation. "Wow, to think how close I was to not bringing this up," I said. "I would have walked away with perceptions that would have kept me stuck with Gabi's red zone."

In response, he offered these nuggets of wisdom:

"Two important things to remember, Kim," he said. "First, women often don't voice those misperceptions. Many times, us guys are not even given a chance to correct it." I agreed, and he continued. "Second, I understand how you were not able to test assumptions like these with men— personally and professionally—earlier in your life. Thank goodness you feel *safe* enough now to see things differently." I nodded in gratitude as he leaned over to kiss me.

"This conversation is so important to the book, Peter. Women can learn how this process unfolds so we catch it. Only then is there a chance for change. Only then can we teach our daughters to think differently," I said. "My struggle with Gabriella's mindset is a big life challenge. This mindset of seeking approval has been a major roadblock in my life."

He paused and lovingly said, "You know how many times we have laughed about why our girl Heather calls so often asking for your advice about what to do? Perhaps she learned it from her mama." Wow. Reality check.

WHAT I COULD NOT SEE

My mind spinning, I went back to work on the final stages of this book. Is this how it happens? Is this how we internalize beliefs that do not serve us or our children? Do we really see the world so differently that instead of testing our assumptions, we simply accept what is not said out loud? Then the silent messages play out day by day. Is this how we end up swimming in the fishbowl with the Narrative? But something was missing. Then it hit me.

Fear.

At the core of my seeking permission and approval was Fear—yet another mean girl of our mindset. Fear loves to remind me of the times I have not made good decisions. Fear makes me wonder if I might screw things up again.

Is Fear interfering with the entire sisterhood? Decide for yourself:

- Is Kari's search for *perfection* masking a deep-seated fear of not being enough?

- Is Ranee's desire to *meet everyone's needs* driven by the fear of letting someone down? Fear of not giving enough?

- Is Gabi's *need for permission or approval* rooted in fear of disappointing someone? Not living up to expectations?

- Is Darsha's need to *accept what is said* simply a cover for fear of judgment, fear of being wrong, or fear of making yet another mistake?

- Was Avalene's thought of *not being qualified enough* simply an attempt to avoid potential disappointment? Deep down, was she hanging out with Kari, fearful of not being enough?

- Surely, Jalila's desire to *work hard and be rewarded* is pure. Or is she also hiding a deeply rooted fear of not having enough, being enough, or doing enough?

- Nikki's desire to *stay in the background* can't be rooted in fear, or can it? What is Nikki afraid of? Is she trying to avoid being rejected? Is she scared someone will discover she is not perfect, along with her sister Kari? Or is she fearful that her light will shine so brightly that the sheer magnitude of her fullness could actually make a difference in the world?

Each of us is called to answer these questions for ourselves. One thing is certain: the red zone of all the sisters begins with Kari's quest for perfection. It ends with her deep profound acceptance of *I am enough*. Deep down, Kari's story is *our* story.

It really is like a web—no beginning, no end—each mindset interconnected.

If we stay close to the red mindsets of the Sisterhood—or continue to ignore what is happening before our very eyes—it will keep us spinning, predictably, in a downward spiral.

If, however, we courageously and *consciously* choose to live life from the green zone of the Sisterhood, we then grow into the real version of who we are, daring to live our fullest life. We will continue to move in a circle, yes. But this time, it will go in an upward direction, propelling us up and forward.

Day by day, decision by decision, we have a choice. What will you choose?

THE POWER OF INTENTION[102]

Before you read this section, close your eyes and take three long, deep, slow breaths. When we take the time to breathe slowly, we send a signal to our bodies that we are safe, which opens a channel to hear ourselves with more clarity. Clear your mind and ask yourself honestly which sister(s) resonates with you. Keep her in mind as you read this section.

Intention is the energy behind the "why" we are saying or doing something. Intention is the unspoken need behind the choice. Two people can take the same action; however, for one person it is *not* the right thing, and for the other person it is. Intention is a small subtle difference that is *everything*—

and it's why so many of us are confused about the messages we receive in the world.

As someone who has battled an eating disorder, intention comes to life for me with something as simple as a piece of chocolate. If I am eating a piece of chocolate because I want to enjoy it, that is fine and healthy. However, if I am eating the same piece of chocolate to fill a void inside—to unconsciously calm an emotion I can't quite recognize or don't want to deal with—then that is something else entirely. It looks the same to the outside world but with a very different meaning on the inside.

Here's another scenario: many of us are facing or will soon face the pressures of caring for an ailing family member. It could be a disabled child, a spouse with an illness, or aging parents. Extreme situations like these are never easy. Many caregivers feel guilty for asking for help. They feel like they *should* be the primary caretaker. This is the Narrative, once again. Add the red zone mindset of Ranee (*I have to meet all demands*) and Kari (*I expect perfection*), and you're on the fast track to the crazy house. It is okay to love yourself enough to draw boundaries. It is okay to ask for help. Instead of caving in to guilt, ask yourself honestly *why* you are seeking help. If it is because you genuinely can't handle it anymore and it is taking a toll on your health, know that it is okay to ask for help. The power lies in understanding the intention behind it. Deeply understanding the intention behind the mindset holds the key to the freedom you desire.

Some people have wondered why "Sisterhood" is not part of the title of this book. The answer is simple: the real message here is about awareness, choosing to make conscious choices and discovering the power that's already within. The Sisterhood is but one way to do that, to shift from living life with the smallness of a meow to the strength of a roar. Living small serves no one.

The Sisterhood is a loving way for each of us to see the world differently. To think differently. To live differently. To embrace our intuitive intelligence. To encourage our sisters—above, beside, and below us—to do the same. One hundred years from now, when our future sisters are taking up the next chapter of empowerment, the Sisterhood they know may be different. But the core message of power, freedom, and love is timeless.

REFLECTION

Consider the car-buying story. Have there been times men or women in your life have said or done things that made you feel powerless? Was it real? Did you test your assumptions? What do you do when these situations arise?

_____

_____

_____

_____

_____

What role does fear play in our living in the red zones of the sisters? How does it show up? What does fear feel like in your body? How do you find the confidence to shift?

_____

_____

_____

_____

_____

BEFORE I KNEW
THE SISTERHOOD

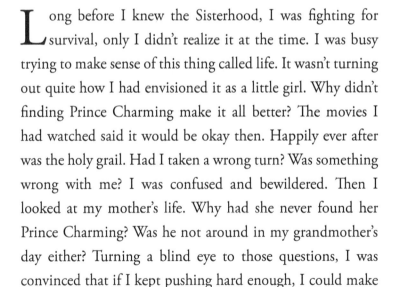

L ong before I knew the Sisterhood, I was fighting for survival, only I didn't realize it at the time. I was busy trying to make sense of this thing called life. It wasn't turning out quite how I had envisioned it as a little girl. Why didn't finding Prince Charming make it all better? The movies I had watched said it would be okay then. Happily ever after was the holy grail. Had I taken a wrong turn? Was something wrong with me? I was confused and bewildered. Then I looked at my mother's life. Why had she never found her Prince Charming? Was he not around in my grandmother's day either? Turning a blind eye to those questions, I was convinced that if I kept pushing hard enough, I could make life turn out like it was supposed to.

After all, now that I had a daughter looking to me for leadership, the stakes were higher than ever. In 2002, I had earned partnership status with a nationally known consulting firm with a clientele of many large corporations. The job required travel, but the family pulled together to manage it. Year after year, my sweet girl was growing. By the time she was four, the realization that I would not have any more children of my own began to sink in. Every moment with my daughter became even more precious as a result.

I remember the day like it was yesterday: Heather was in third grade, and mornings had become a bit of a struggle. I would try to pull her hair back for school, and she would refuse. *I am too cool for hair bows*, she would adamantly tell me. I searched for substitutes to the traditional hair bow. Back in those days, there were limited options. In my desperation to find an alternative that would bring peace to our mornings, I made a simple hair ornament with a ponytail

holder and long ribbons. Heather loved it. She affectionately called them Sassytails—they made her feel sassy, and they had tails. Voilà—our morning problem was solved. Little did I know what was to come.

As Heather wore these simple ornamental hair accessories, friends at school started to ask for them. My weekends became filled with assembling accessories for her to share. Much to our surprise, other moms started to call and request these "darling accessories." Wherever Heather and I would travel, moms would stop us on the street and ask us where to buy the product in Heather's hair. By the time a local cheerleading squad requested an order, Heather was filled with ideas of her own. *"Mom, I have a great idea. We should start a business together and call it Sassy-tails,"* she said, going on to explain that it would give us more time together so I would not have to travel so much. *"I will be vice president,"* she declared. Everyone told me I was crazy. *What a "hair"brained idea!* they would declare, pun intended. *Why are you even considering it?* While I continued to work full time, Heather and I started our small company, using our dining room table for the production line.

By that point, I had started to recognize the messages the world was giving to girls about how they had to look and act a certain way. I heard similar messages growing up, but now my daughter's future was at stake. It made me see the world differently. I did the research and learned that over $50 million worth of ponytail holders per year were sold in the United States alone. Suddenly, I began to wonder if there was something to this idea. Was it possible to create a company that could inspire girls to realize they were beautiful the way they were? Could Heather and I set an example for others that girls could create a very different future than what was expected?

In summer 2004, we tested the concept at a kiosk in Myrtle Beach, South Carolina. I figured the test market would allow Heather and me time together while inspiring her to dream big. I also thought it would show that the idea did not have enough merit to move forward. Boy, was I wrong! We discovered that moms from all over the country were evidently having the same issue. People were inspired by a seven-year-old vice president and mother-daughter entrepreneur team. By the end of the summer, I boldly took the leap.[103] I knew this was going to be my only child, and I was determined to show her that dreams can come true.

In 2004, we officially launched our company called Sassytails,[104] fueled by a shared dream to change the way girls saw themselves and the world. Slowly, we grew from having our products sold in twenty stores to one hundred stores. Our products were in Atlanta, Chicago, Dallas, and Los Angeles showrooms. The story was compelling. As we grew, it became evident that the dream was taking on a life of its own. I started to seek investors so we could scale the dream and broaden our reach. Keep in mind that the internet was in its infancy back then. The only way to grow was to sell product to retailers. Trade show after trade show,[105] the interest and orders grew. My quest for investors became critical as it would take a while for the profitability to scale so I could take a salary. A deadline was set by the husband at the time. Find investors by *X*, or give up this crazy idea and find a real job with a steady paycheck. For months, I ran parallel tracks, knowing time was running out. The pressure at home was mounting for a multitude of reasons. I would search for jobs in the morning and run Sassytails in the afternoon. I knew I could make a difference, but things were not happening fast enough. *Push harder,* I told myself. It came down to the last week of the deadline I was given. I had a follow-up interview with an agency for a job I was likely to be offered. My head said, "Give up the dream and just take the job." My heart was crying for something very different. I scheduled my last opportunity for investors the same afternoon. My spirit torn, I had come to the end of the road.

The morning of November 15, 2005, arrived. The 10:00 a.m. interview was with the board of directors of the agency. It went well, and it became clear I was a good fit. The chairman of the board had not been able to attend at the last minute, but the team assured me that they would fill him in. I left the interview and listened to voice mails. More orders for Sassytails. My heart could barely stand it. *God, what do you want from me?* I asked.

The 3:00 p.m. investor meeting finally arrived. With heartfelt consideration, I gave it my all. I was supposed to meet with only one investor, but he had unexpectedly invited another gentleman to attend. An hour and a half later, the meeting came to a close. Both men had daughters and were inspired by my vision to create a company that would positively influence girls. The second potential investor excused himself, saying he was due at an agency meeting—he had missed an important interview earlier that morning. We were able to put two and two together. He was the absent chairman of the board from my interview, and I was the important interview he had missed. "Oh no," he said. "If we invest in Sassytails, you won't be able to take the job." The synchronicity surprised us all.

I drove home and waited. I said to the husband, "Whichever one comes through is a sign of the right path." At 6:00 p.m., the phone rang. It was the agency with a generous job offer. I said I would reply in the morning. Every ounce of my being had been hoping for a different call. While the husband was relieved that this ridiculous business idea would soon be over, I continued to hold out hope.

At 9:00 p.m., the phone rang again. It was the potential investors offering my full request for $300,000 to take Sassy-tails to the next level. I hung up and wept. Heather and I jumped for joy at our dream becoming a reality. I fought the Narrative being demanded of me. Nothing would stop us now—or so I thought.

Fueled with an investment, momentum, and enough passion to take on the world, our journey continued. I hired talented women who believed in our vision to support the growing demand. Soon our products were being sold in four hundred stores, then six hundred. Our ability to manufacture the product through our cottage network was no longer enough. We secured overseas manufacturing and broadened our product line along the way, including consumer product licenses from Warner Brothers and Disney. Heather led the creation of a junior advisory board, including young girls who participated in many of our business decisions. We were both deeply committed to creating a company *for* girls and *by* girls. We were on our way to building a brand that would positively influence the way girls saw themselves and the world.

I could see the impact being a vice president in the third grade was having on Heather's life. I still have the elementary school collage of artwork that were important to her. Right in the middle is her Sassytails business card. By that point, she had been part of product development, worked our booth at trade shows, and made presentations to investors. Despite what some people said, there was no telling Heather[106] that she was vice president in name only. It changed her perspective of the world and made her believe she could do anything.

The entire Sassytails experience was a testament to the power of a vision. It was my first foray into creating my own path and learning to trust my own decisions. We all worked extremely hard, and the learning curve was steep. I still faced numerous battles on the home front, torn between doing what I was told I should do and doing what I knew I was *called* to do. Little did I know it was not wise to fight internal battles and external battles at the same time. I believed I was invincible. It turns out, I wasn't.

WHEN A DREAM BECOMES A NIGHTMARE

To this day, it is not easy for me to explain how it all came crashing down. The only way I can describe it is to say there was a perfect storm of circumstances. The success and level of growth[107] was more than our small company could stand. Blinded by a dream, I was not able to see it at the time. A major investor had undiagnosed Alzheimer's, which led to decisions with serious implications. One of those decisions involved a potential investor with malicious intent. For nine months, I desperately fought to save the company but ended up a statistic of the economic crash of 2008.[108] I was searching for change to buy a gallon of gas (a story I shared earlier in the book). The year ended with me declaring bankruptcy personally and professionally. Words cannot express how heartbreaking it was to tell my very young vice president that sometimes dreams don't come true. My attempt to break free from the Narrative turned into a nightmare.

I lost everything this world teaches us is important. Even more devastating, I lost my passion for life. I lost my belief in the goodness of people. I even stopped believing God was good. I gave up on my dreams and resigned myself to merely existing. I branded myself with a big *F* on my forehead: *F* for *failure*. I lost my confidence, the ability to trust my judgment, and my desire to connect with other people. I did what I had to do to make it through each day, trying to be a mother to my precious girl.

My days were gray. Years passed.

Shortly after Heather turned twelve, she began asking me tough questions that were wise beyond her age. *Why are you doing that? Why do you put up with that? Why don't you stand up for what you really believe?* She would hold me accountable for why I said one thing and did another. Her insights and observations continued to such a degree that I was shocked at what I was *really* teaching my daughter. I had made a lot of progress, but wow, I still had a long way to go.

As moms, we genuinely believe we are teaching our children the right lessons. We underestimate the impact of the incongruence of our messages. If our words say one thing but our actions say another, what do our daughters and sons really take away? When our actions and words are not in sync, there is a space—a confusing emptiness, a chasm, a question not answered. When this happens over and over again, our children answer the question unconsciously, and it becomes part of their DNA of thought—it establishes certain patterns that significantly affect life moving forward. Remember the one-hundred-year-old narrative with which we started our journey earlier? How "old" mindsets are still tucked away in the DNA of our thoughts? Evidently, I had some tucked away too.

For me, Sassytails represented a chance to do something meaningful while claiming my independence. I had watched family members remain trapped by not having independence, which significantly limited their choices, and it frightened me. When my efforts failed, I came face to face with the belief that maybe the family had been right: life really is stacked against you, and you should just swallow the bitter pill and give up dreams of a better life. The DNA of thought that we are powerless to influence the outcome of our lives was killing my spirit. It seemed as if I were doomed to repeat the past.

My mother, a stay-at-home mom for thirteen years, was catapulted unexpectedly into a working world for which she was not prepared. Scrambling to earn an associate's degree, she pressed on to figure out how to support herself and the family. The years following the divorce were frightening and traumatic for everyone involved. This event, which happened when she was thirty-three years old—almost thirty-seven years ago—still affects her today as she faces retirement. It is a sobering reminder of cause and effect being far removed in space and time. I had a close-up view of the life of my mother, a fellow sister, driven by the mindsets of the generation before her. They taught her to believe someone would take care of her. They taught her to look outside of herself for the answers.

The experience drove me to vow: *I will always be able to support myself.* This is a mental model, which has been a blessing and a curse in my life as well as in the life of my daughter. The challenges my mother and I had in our relationship were driven by a difference of perspective. Every time there was an emotional exchange, I was reminded of the importance of my work to shift the way I think so life would be different for my daughter.

For those of you who have faced numerous challenges growing up, perhaps you can relate. There were no picture-perfect family memories. There was little money for college education, much less advanced degrees. There were no opportunities without scratching and fighting for every cent. I vividly remember wanting to blame everyone else—God, society, social norms, family—for not providing opportunities others had. It took me a *long* time to learn that blame serves no one.[109] I was at war with myself. I screamed at the heavens, *"I did not know better, damn it!"*

The divine answer I received was simple: "You did not know then, but you do know now. Now is the only thing that matters. You have two choices, Kimberly: Victimhood or victory. It is that simple. Despite the hardships and things out of  your control, you also made choices that brought you to this place today. You can choose a new path. The cage you have placed yourself in has no back. Step out, dear one, and live the life you were meant to live."

I thought back to all the times I had second-guessed myself, said what I thought everyone else wanted to hear, and pushed down deep what I really needed. As agonizing as it was to accept, I had indeed played a role in my own disaster.

Even with the insight, I was paralyzed by fear. I was caught up in the shoulds, judgment of myself, and judgment from others. There were many well-meaning "religious" women who told me where my place was supposed to be. They frightened me by warning of the huge mistakes I would make by leaving the marriage and changing my life. I came face to face with a major intersection of life: Victimhood or victory, right?

In 2011, I finally made the heartbreaking decision to move forward with a divorce. Having been paralyzed by the fact that I did not want to repeat the toxic divorce of my parents, it was life changing to realize I could do it differently. I did not have to repeat the toxic patterns of the past. Determined to create a different experience, I did everything I could to move forward with compassion. I chose to leave with $4,500 to my name, a few pieces of furniture, and not much else to show for twenty years of marriage, except, of course, my beloved daughter—the light of my life. My love for her carried me when love for myself did not.

LIVING (AND FIGHTING TO LIVE) THE LIFE I WAS MEANT TO LIVE

Every year after the divorce, I faced battles. Each year I grew stronger. Whenever the failure of Sassytails threatened to defeat me, I reminded myself to keep moving forward—day by day, decision by decision. Any time I was tempted to look externally for the answer, I shifted my focus to the power inside and ignited the power within first. I chose to trust the process in the hope that someday it would all make sense. When my inside changed—and I mean truly changed—everything shifted.

The real proof for me today is watching my twenty-two-year-old daughter view the world very differently. While her narrative is still being written, I have seen evidence that she is close friends with the green zone of the Sisterhood. Back in 2013, my mental model of the Sassytails experience was a complete failure. Heather taught me to see it differently when she completed an essay on an application for a math and science school when she was fifteen years old. Here are her words:

"I have been in the business world since I was six, when my mom and I started a company called Sassytails. At eight years old, I spoke to hundreds of high school students about entrepreneurship.[110] I worked with a media team to write a script and star in a Harry Potter video[111] for our company. ...

"Our story was even featured in the *Wall Street Journal*.[112]

"Launching this company, I learned how much work it takes to create something you really want. Despite our success, our investor team made some mistakes, which led us to make hard business decisions. These mistakes led to the closing of Sassytails. I was 11 years old.

"Through this experience, I learned not only about the business world, but also how to fail with grace. [That was the sentence that made me cry!] Learning about failure at a young age has shaped the person I am today. It has made me not afraid of it. In my opinion, it is a part of life that everyone goes through. I consider myself lucky this whole Sassytails experience has made me not afraid of any challenge."

Sometimes it is from our children that we learn the most. My daughter sees the world through a different lens, and for that I am grateful.

My new life today is very different because I am a different person—emotionally, physically, spiritually, and energetically. This new life has taught me that the sisters are like us: multidimensional. When I thought I knew the green zone of Jalila by owning my value at work, she showed me that there is an entirely different dimension to owning your value when blending two families together. The learning continues.

When we do the work and go the distance with these mental models, the world comes into focus. When we see the Narrative playing out, we can say to ourselves, *I don't think so, sister. Not going there today.* And then, driven by the love we have for others, we are *compelled* to spread the message. You want other women to experience the freedom too.

CIRCLE OF LIFE: REWRITING OUR PERSONAL NARRATIVE FIRST

During those difficult years, I was trapped by the red zones of many of the sisters. I remember in vivid detail what it was like. The expectation of perfection was my constant companion. It seemed that everywhere I turned, I wasn't enough. I was overwhelmed by doing everything I thought I *had* to do. I was constantly seeking approval, only I did not realize that consciously. I apologized for breathing oxygen and even taking up space on the planet. I was convinced that everyone else's opinion was more important than my own. I told myself to accept the status quo, even when everything inside me was screaming otherwise. The list goes on and on. What was the collective impact of drowning in the red zone? **I gave away my personal power.** Like Dorothy in ruby slippers walking down the yellow brick road,[113] I had the power all along, but I could not see it at the time.

Through my journey with the Sisterhood, I made three life-altering, powerful discoveries. These discoveries resulted in a transformation of my life and my purpose.

1. **Shift to the offensive.** There is a big difference between being on the defensive and being on the offensive, much like the difference between Victimhood and victory. Every decision we make is driven by feeling powerless or powerful. Each decision is rooted in fear or love.[114] Yet we don't often slow down long enough to ask ourselves the question. Every time I was facing a battle, fear always led me to a defensive position, a powerless place to be. The only time I was able to gain ground was when I stepped into an offensive mindset and shifted to the energy of love—even if it was simply love for myself. Love propels us forward. When I stepped into powerful mindsets, the fears grew smaller. When I stopped fueling the fear, it lost its luster. Drama, Powerlessness, and Just faded into the background. When I changed internally, everything externally began to change.

2. **Respect is an inside job first.** Once I stopped giving in to fear, I was startled to find that the world responded. When I respected myself and owned the power that had been inside all along, everyone—including men— started to treat me differently. The sheer vibration and life force I radiated set in motion a very different reality. All of it was driven by my mental models. The beliefs I had internally were unconsciously driving

the conversation. The more I lived in the green zone, the language I chose to use changed the direction of each interaction. I reached a place where I would not, could not tolerate disrespect on any level. I started to boldly claim my value one small step at a time. Guess what? Others started to respond. That is when the aha became crystal clear. Changing my external world required me to change my internal world first. As within, so without.

That understanding also led my perspective of men to shift. Instead of viewing them as the enemy or as ones to be feared—as life and the Narrative had taught me—I learned to embrace the true partnerships we can have together. The offensive mindset I chose for myself changed everything. If I was not respected, then I removed myself from the situation. All of a sudden, they realized this was no longer an optional game. It was either give the respect I was due or ... wait, there was no "or." It was either respect or nothing.

There is a fine line to walk when it comes to stepping into our power *and* working with the other 50 percent of humanity we know as our sons, husbands, brothers, friends, and colleagues. Results matter to men. It is really much simpler than we realize. We can learn to speak their language—a language rooted in results. They can learn to speak our language as well. They will treat us with respect when we give it to ourselves first—and then demand it—in a calmly confident, calmly passionate manner.

The unintended consequence of our tolerating disrespectful behavior for so long is that in effect we have had a hand in training them to not take us seriously. While we are shifting the way we think to stop accepting the unacceptable,[115] it is important that we don't allow the pendulum to swing to a male-bashing culture. As women, we are designed to birth, to create. And that means creating a culture of love and acceptance. Tough love, yes, but love nevertheless. We don't have to subject ourselves to poor behavior by anyone.

Many are encouraging us to have different conversations about this very issue. Joanne Lipman, author of *That's What She Said*,[116] speaks passionately as she states, "When men and women work together toward a common goal, great things can happen. All of us are better off for it." Men and women are in this boat called life together. It serves no one for one side or the other to be beaten down. This is a critical understanding in the circle of life. Yes, the masculine leadership principle is out of alignment, and it is holding humanity hostage via a state of chaos and confusion. That we can't control. A way to change the momentum and stop the downward spiral is for the feminine leadership principle to rise up in equal strength. This we *can* control. Day by day, decision by decision.

More to come about the feminine leadership principle at MyIntuitiveIntelligence.com

3. **Create a life of choice.** When we have choices, we have power. There are a multitude of reasons why many women have not been able to create a life of choice; however, we are entering a time when we can change that reality. We have the ability to tune in to our intuitive intelligence, which we have been taught to ignore for far too long. We will be guided by our wisdom when we start tapping into our inner-net far more than the internet.

    We are at the precipice of a tipping point for the empowerment of women and a very different reality for all. Having the freedom to walk away from disrespect speaks volumes—personally and professionally. When we stop investing time banging our heads against the wall of his-story, we free up the emotional energy to write her-story one page at a time. And her-story naturally evolves into OUR story.

    I am convinced that hope for humanity is trapped in the hearts of women. When that hope is harnessed, the world will evolve into a profoundly uplifting experience for all.

    This is all possible in your world too. Yes, there is a razor-thin line between giving in and leaning in. The temptation to give in is not what defines us. The choice we make at that intersection does.

REFLECTION

Has there been a time in your life when you placed yourself in a cage with no back? What was the circumstance? If you were to zoom out and see it from a different perspective, could you recognize the sisters with whom you might be dancing?

What do you think about the phrase the "DNA of thought"? What are some of the thoughts that were passed down to you professionally or personally? Is it time to rewrite them so you can live your fullest life?

What commitment do you want to make to yourself today as you move into the green zones of freedom?

WHEN WE ARE TEMPTED TO GIVE IN

The Narrative can feel like quicksand drawing us in. The more we fight, the deeper we sink. We grow tired of fighting the status quo and wonder if things will ever change. How can we still be fighting issues like sexual harassment in the workplace? Weren't those battles supposed to be won decades ago? Weren't we liberated when *The Feminine Mystique*[117] started a revolution in 1963? We wonder if our small actions even matter. After all, we are but one person. We wonder about the futures of our daughters, granddaughters, nieces, and the young women we mentor.

The exhaustion is real. The weariness is tedious.

There are times when giving in instead of leaning in seems like the only realistic alternative. When you find yourself at that intersection—wondering if your actions matter—know that they do matter. Take heart in knowing that *you* matter.

Every time we pause, reflect, and consciously choose our direction, we create a new reality—individually and collectively. The answers we seek will never lie outside of us. Yes, we stand on each other's shoulders as we build on our successes, but ultimately, the answer is within. This book defines the concept of tapping into your power. You have the ability to ignite—to discover—your power and live your fullest life. Seeing through the Narrative and embracing the power of the Sisterhood for our own lives first is the key that will unlock the collective shift we desire. When we change our inner dialogue—and what we see in the mirror each day—the collective power to create a world that truly values women will follow.

Look in the mirror right now. The reflection you see—your lion inside—has the power to change the world. That is the Truth, and Truth will always change the landscape we know as reality.

This is the grand adventure beckoning to us all.

WHAT IS TRULY AT STAKE?

Let us be very aware of what is truly at stake. On February 23, 2017, I was leading a three-day training program for a group of corporate women identified as high-potential leaders for a global company of 180,000 employees. We were in a quaint village a few kilometers outside Paris, France. For three days, we worked on enhancing their executive presence, building their leadership brand, and improving their overall communication skills. As with many similar sessions before, the bulk of the work was in reminding each of them how talented they really were. The Narrative had done quite a job of dimming the light within. My job was to be a mirror that allowed each of these women to see in themselves what I could so clearly see: accomplished women with an unbelievable amount of power waiting to be unleashed.

The last day of the program came, and Aki, a talented young woman from India, was preparing to present a speech. Throughout our time together, I had noticed an unusual characteristic in Aki: any time she had something to say, she would simply start talking and wouldn't stop until everyone else in the room had no choice but to be quiet. I was confounded about how to address it. As I was helping Aki get ready to go out on stage and give her presentation, I asked her about this communication technique. In those few moments, I could see and feel the intense fear surrounding that subject for her. She was having difficulty articulating why she communicated in that manner. In that awkward moment of silence, I finally understood what was really happening.

That characteristic—the very one that the rest of us in the session were mystified by—was a sign of strength where she was from. It was what she had to do every single day to even have a chance to be heard.

She literally had to steamroll over the men in her culture simply to get a word in edgewise. It was the only way she ever had a voice. But time did not allow for reflection; it was time for her to present to the class.

Aki walked slowly to the front of the room to begin her presentation. As she started to speak, her voice began to shake, and the tears started to fall. She was visibly unnerved by our conversation. No one spoke a word. My heart was breaking with hers. It was a moment of truth unlike any other I had experienced in my twenty years of training. The class was bewildered about what was unfolding. After a moment of heartfelt consideration, I walked onstage, stood next to Aki, and told the class about our conversation.

Then the magic happened.

I watched as this group of women from seven different countries came together to support Aki in that moment of uncertainty. Anne, a brave leader from the United Kingdom, said with absolute conviction, "Aki, we know you don't have this kind of support in your world, but I want you to know you have it right now. And it does not have to stop with this training class. You are one of us, and we are right here to encourage you every step of the way." The powerful commentary continued. For the first time in her life, Aki was experiencing a professional Sisterhood. She took a deep breath and composed herself. Emboldened by the strength of the women surrounding and supporting her, Aki delivered her presentation with power. It was an amazing moment that transcended age, race, and nationality, defined by the transformational power of Sisterhood. It is a Sisterhood that truly has the power to change the world, one woman at a time.

On the long flight home, as I was replaying the powerful moments of the program in my mind, it all became crystal clear. I now knew what was truly at stake. I finally understood what the Sisterhood had been trying to tell me all along.

> It is of great significance that we magnify the power of women in countries where we are free so it will be amplified, resulting in a tsunami of liberation for women around the world.

If we don't fully embrace that power and our voice, then what hope do others around the world have who are fighting much bigger battles? We are part of a larger collective story playing out day after day across the world. When we find ourselves tempted to give in instead of lean in, think of Aki and women like her around the world. Every single day, we can choose to embrace the power available to us.

We are lucky to have it.

Interested in learning more about women's empowerment around the world? Here is additional recommended reading:

Betraying Big Brother: The Feminist Awakening in China, by Leta Hong Fincher[119]

Fifty Million Rising: The New Generation of Working Women Transforming the Muslim World, by Saadia Zahidi[120]

#globalsisterhood

THE LEVERAGE

The surprising leverage inherent in this entire book is that women are more than willing to go the distance for others.[121]

When we can't muster up enough love for ourselves, we tap into the deep reservoir of love we have for others. Fear can be a barrier to us personally; however, courage bubbles up from the depths of our soul when it comes to protecting someone—or something—else. Think mama bear syndrome on steroids. The group Moms Demand Action for Gun Sense in America is one example of many of what can happen when women courageously fight for their families. As Shannon Watts, founder of Moms Demand Action and author of *Fight Like a Mother*,[122] says, "Women have been the secret sauce in the progress we've made on many social issues throughout time."

Whether it is the passion we have for our families, our children, our pets, or for humanity, this legacy of love is powerful enough to redefine the Narrative as we know it today. The feminine principle of leadership defends the interests of the whole. It embraces the power of networks and connection. It invites collaboration instead of competition. There has never been a more important moment for this type of leadership to rise to the forefront.

The time is now.

#reWritetheNarrative

ORGANIZATIONS CAN'T DO IT ALONE

Every time we read a workplace report on diversity, we are seeing through only one lens—the lens of his story. It does not give us a clear picture of reality. The sobering truth is that if every diversity and gender equality initiative were 100 percent successful, we would inevitably run into the reality that our *internal dialogue* is still standing in the way. Every woman's story in this book, and countless others, are living holograms of this reality. However, once women changed their internal mindsets, everything shifted. **It is an inside job first.**

Yes, corporations need to continue probing into the inequities. Yes, we need to continue partnering with men to create new realities for us all. Let us not lose sight of the fact that there are many good men out there fighting for us as well. Having said that, yes, sexual harassment must be rooted out at every level. Many of the distorted expectations that have been considered normal are beginning to be dismantled, brick by brick; however, our work—individually and collectively—is just beginning. We are at the precipice of a ceiling-shattering window of time, watching as the shift unfolds with momentum many of us thought we would never see in our lifetimes. Whether it is the powerful testimony of American female gymnasts who were abused by the predatory doctor Larry Nassar[123] or the story of Rania Fahmy,[124] a young woman in Egypt who fought a male attacker physically and in court, the world is significantly changing. Each time justice was driven by a woman who shifted her internal perspective *first* to ignite a wave of change. We have a front-row seat to what happens when those who have abused their power are held accountable.

THIS IS NOT A NEW STORY

People abusing power is not a new story.

It is important to understand a key reason Susan B. Anthony fought so hard for the right to vote. She and her fellow warriors were heartbroken over women who were abused—emotionally and physically. There were many stories of her sheltering women and children who were fleeing domestic violence—much of it driven by alcohol abuse. She knew women would remain powerless if they could not influence policy at every level.

Think about the significance of this for a moment.

The suffrage movement was driven by a desire to give women power over their lives and by the belief that the answers to their troubles would come from society and from those in power. The writings of these suffragettes reveal their genuine belief that fighting for the right to vote would solve the issues facing women. They had every reason to think the answer was external. However, if that were true, then why are we living with our current reality and with the following statistics nearly a hundred years later?

- Nearly one in four women in the United States has experienced severe physical violence by an intimate partner in her lifetime.[125] Fifty American women are shot and killed by intimate partners each month.

- More than half of all American women—54 percent—have experienced "unwanted and inappropriate sexual advances" at some point in their lives, according to a recent poll; 33 million US women have been sexually harassed in work-related episodes.[126]

- In the United States[127] and abroad,[128] one in four young people don't think it's serious if a guy who is normally gentle sometimes slaps his girlfriend when he's drunk and they're arguing.[129]

The statistics provide a snapshot of reality. In many cases, the statistics for our sisters globally are even more heartbreaking. Perhaps there is an additional sobering dynamic at play in this larger story. Is it possible that we have invested so much of our emotional bandwidth into looking outside of ourselves—for power, for blame, shifting from one defensive move to another—that we have missed opportunities to significantly shift the internal dialogue of which the Sisterhood speaks?

Is it possible that once we embrace the empowering mindsets each sister has revealed to us, we will shift our internal expectations to such a degree that we will not be able to tolerate the pervasive disrespect at the heart of the troubling statistics? Can you consider the possibility that today we are facing a crossroads of epic proportions where we have a chance to change our future by shifting our internal dialogues?

I believe it is quite possible.

This brings us right back to where we are today—a world away from a generation ago. In many ways, we *have* changed women's reality:

- *The Feminine Mystique*, a best-selling book by Betty Friedan published in 1963, was crucial in explaining "that which has no name"—the prevailing belief that as a woman, fulfillment had only one definition: housewife-mother. It was a watershed moment igniting a wave of change that rippled through society. Coincidentally, the book *Lean In* was released fifty years later—also igniting another wave of change, one in which we each have a front-row seat.

- Women's participation in the US labor force has climbed from 32.7 percent in 1948 to 56.8 percent in 2016.[130]

- The proportion of women with college degrees in the labor force has almost quadrupled since 1970. More than 57 percent of women in the labor force had college degrees in 2016–2017, compared with 11 percent in 1970.[131]

- The range of occupations female workers hold has also expanded, with women making notable gains in professional and managerial positions.[132]

- Efforts to increase women in STEM (science, technology, engineering, and math) are actively addressing the issue that only 35 percent of undergraduate degrees in engineering go to women.[133]

- Storybooks and toys for girls are dismantling stereotypes by expanding to include what were traditionally seen as boys' interests.[134]

- Even a tradition like the Girl Scouts is experiencing profound changes—which comes as no surprise since the new CEO, Sylvia Acevedo, is literally a rocket scientist.[135] New badges in science, cybersecurity, coding, and citizenship are paving the way for a very different future for our girls.[136]

All of this is good news. But the real question is, why are we still tolerating disrespectful behavior—personally or professionally?

The answer: the Narrative has convinced us that we have to.

We have been listening to the Narrative for so long that we can't even see what her-story might look like. Here is a glimpse into the future—*if we choose:*

- Instead of sexual harassment training that instills fear in the workplace, we invite our men to be part of the training. Imagine asking each dad to explain to his daughter face to face what kind of treatment she should expect in the workplace. Is it possible that fathers and daughters are the gateway to a new understanding for men? Fear is never enough for sustainable change. Love is.

- When we negotiate a salary, we *all* are asking questions about pay equity, flexibility, and a workplace free from sexual harassment. If the job requires travel, we ask whether we will be supported to stay in hotels that are safe. We boldly ask for the higher salary— remembering our sisters like Aki—knowing that when we negotiate for one, we negotiate for all.

- We bravely bring to light any behavior that does not respect us, individually or collectively. We create a life of choice that allows us to pursue other options as needed. Results are what matter to those in power. When we stop choosing to allow our blood, sweat, and tears to make them more money, therefore giving them more power, then things will begin to change. When disrespectful behavior rears its head, we now have the tools to collectively say stop to ignite change:

  Shout
  To the world
  Our collective
  Power to drive change

- We have conversations with our daughters and the young women we mentor, painting a new vision for the future. We make a conscious choice to refuse to keep the Narrative alive by giving its tired old story lines any more power; instead, we focus our energy on writing her-story. It takes effort to **stop repeating the Narrative**, with all of its negative statistics. It is important to remember that what we focus on grows. **Each time you speak, consciously choose to tell a new story, and stop giving power to the old Narrative.**

- We boldly step out on behalf of all sisters when it comes to negotiating salaries, hiring suppliers, and elevate any opportunity that arises to achieve pay equity for all of us. May the story of the joint salary negotiations by actresses Jessica Chastain and Octavia Spencer inspire us to think and behave differently.[137]

- We encourage our sons, husbands, friends, and coworkers—all the men in our world—to understand that to receive the respect they crave, treating others with respect first is the key. Remember, men have their own Narrative to dismantle. Thought leaders and authors like Jackson Katz[138] and Warren Farrell and John Gray[139] are bringing much-needed awareness to this issue.

We can draw boundaries with men while still caring for them. As women, we are designed for tough love and fully equipped to be love warriors for humanity.[140]

We are entering a golden age of transparency and respect.[141] We are entering an era where we can no longer live a divided life, where we are one person in front of the world and another behind closed doors. Where we are one person in the professional world and another at home. We are each being offered an opportunity for the alignment of our true selves, therefore strengthening our personal power. The universe is calling us to bring to light that which has been standing in the shadows. The good news is that there is freedom on the other side. Despite how it might appear at first glance, this is an exciting time for humanity. It is a time that offers each of us an open invitation to rewrite the Narrative.

Literally and figuratively, humanity depends on it.

INFLUENCING THE DNA OF THOUGHT

The Sisterhood reminds us that the pervasive Powerlessness holding us back is anchored by one thing: **what we believe about ourselves**.

It is the subtle nuances that are still tucked away in the DNA of our thoughts that are affecting us now. Many women are on autopilot, blinded to our own power to change how we see the world. The limiting thoughts show up in unexpected, unconscious, and silent ways. This book is my attempt to map out the misfiring in the DNA sequence still affecting women today. You are an atom of change. It is within our grasp to shift the DNA of thought so it will positively influence generations to come. Consciously choose to unplug from the Narrative.

Lessen your dependence[142] on TV, movies, your phone, and social media. Start tuning in to your intuitive intelligence. Trust the wisdom coming from your inner-net instead of the internet. Shift your focus from what everyone has told you your world has to be to what it *could* be. Redefine it on your own terms. Shift from breaking the rules to *making* the rules.

The significance of your life and your personal power is transformational—individually and collectively. The world is ripe for this alchemy of thought.[143]

> Beliefs we have accepted as the way things are have been unraveling. To learn more about this topic, read:
>
> *The Hacking of the American Mind,* by Robert H. Lustig[144]
> *How to Break Up with Your Phone,* by Catherine Price[145]
>
> *Inferior: How Science Got Women Wrong— and the New Research That's Rewriting the Story,* by Angela Saini[146]
>
> And as we move into an era of artificial intelligence, a key element of the emerging story we all need to be aware of is highlighted in *Brotopia: Breaking Up the Boys' Club of Silicon Valley,* by Emily Chang. It is

important to learn how disrespect is baked into the system in the world of technology, as it influences so much of our lives. Become more aware so you make more conscious decisions.[147]

The generations before us had little choice but to see the world through his-story; however, we live in an unprecedented time when we don't have to. Remember the teenager-versus-toddler example, where the system grew up but the mindsets did not? It is time for our mindsets to consciously catch up. We are at a crossroads. We can choose to set his-story aside and ask ourselves each day with each choice, "What could her-*story* look like?" Remember, it naturally evolves into *our story* because that is how women are innately designed. It is my deep desire that we will not need to have these same conversations one hundred years from now. And that means we need to embrace new ways of thinking today.

It is important to be aware of when someone else's narrative is coming out of your mouth. Whenever we find ourselves uttering the word *should*, know it is a signal that the Narrative is tap dancing in your subconscious. Start asking *why* about everything—internally and externally. Enter into a process of discovery. You will be surprised at how much of our world—and our dialogue—is driven by beliefs and practices that *are no longer relevant*. As women, we are wired for these times of enormous change. The ability to maneuver is built into our DNA. Boldly embrace it and step into your power.

The only way we will create a culture that truly values women is to embrace collective change and individual change with *equal intensity*. But know that individual change always comes first. Individual change is the catalyst. I learned this firsthand—and so can you.

CHANGE IS A CONTINUUM

In today's world, so many want a formula, a template, five easy steps to the end goal. However, the journey to finding your lion inside is very different for each of us. It's a journey that involves change, and there's no formula for that. Change is a continuum that allows space for a new reality to be revealed. We can't control the changes, but we can empty the toxicity in our life and make room for the new and good. We can't see her-story when we are so busy managing his-story. We cannot shift to an offensive position in life as long as we are on the defensive. We cannot start thriving until we move past surviving. A new reality cannot emerge when our current reality is overflowing with judgment—from ourselves or from others.

TEN YEARS AGO

Ten years ago, I was in survival mode, drowning in the red zone. This is what my lion inside meant to me then:

Limit the damage others can do to me

Independence—find it!

Own my yes

Now is the only time that matters

FIVE YEARS AGO

I was newly divorced and learning to simplify life. I was starting to unplug from the Narrative. I made a conscious choice to detach from the drama. I started to move into the yellow zone of many of the sisters.

Live

Inspired

Own my

New story

TODAY

I have now been living in the green zone of freedom for years. I now see the Narrative very clearly. I powerfully choose a new reality for myself every day.

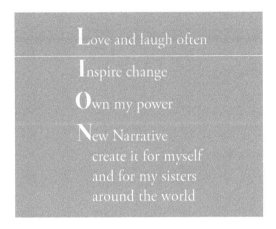

Love and laugh often

Inspire change

Own my power

New Narrative
create it for myself
and for my sisters
around the world

I don't know what my lion inside will mean to me in ten years. The journey continues. What story is your lion inside inviting you to write today?

Your heart knows. Dare to listen.

L _____

I _____

O _____

N _____

WE ARE THE HERO WE SEEK

You may wonder if the sisters will ever go away. Will there be a time when a mindset holding us back will be gone for good?

Some sisters go away once we have learned all we need from them. Like loved ones we have lost, we hold onto the lessons they shared with us. And we remain grateful they were a part of our lives.

Other sisters will be with us for a lifetime, and we become better at bringing out their best. When a challenging situation arises, threatening to bring back the old mindsets, we cycle through it faster. Today, in the company of the Sisterhood, what took two years to process before now takes only two days. You'll be able to quickly recognize the mindsets that no longer serve you much faster, and you will *consciously* choose a different mindset. Therein lies the power of the Sisterhood for the rest of your life.

As for me, I am now thankful for the Sassytails experience. It was the leverage for me to live my fullest life. It taught me who I was when everything I knew was stripped from me. Everything was brought into question. My ability to trust my judgment about others and myself was shattered. Faith in my future was nonexistent. I set out to discover who I was without all of the trappings I had called "my life." Who I was without money, without a title. Who I was with no story.

When it comes to failure, there is such a thing as hitting rock bottom. When you cannot disappoint people any more than you've already disappointed them. When you cannot shatter expectations any more than they are already shattered. A place where there is truly nowhere to go but up—and surprisingly, that's a freeing realization. No matter what, the sun comes up every day. As we learn to embrace Kari's message of *I am enough*, we find great strength. That strength gives us the courage to be vulnerable and to share our stories … failures and all. There is great value in those experiences despite—and sometimes because of—their not-so-great endings. People need to know there is life beyond failure, whether it is personal or professional. We must help each other remember that as long as we have the ability to love, we can make a difference in this world. The rest can be overcome with time.

We build these stories into our lives, and we live them out. *Things are okay,* we tell ourselves, *as long as we live out the script.* But when the story is shattered—the pages ripped out of the storybook, leaving us with nothing but a tattered cover—we ask in bewilderment, *What now?* To my sisters who have been there, you know of what I speak.

You set out on a journey to figure out what matters. It took a while to accept the notion that as long as I could give another human being a hug, life was worth living. If I could offer one word of encouragement to another, that was enough. Without money. Without the trappings of success we are taught is the goal. Without prestige, power, or fame, I was enough. I could still be a wonderful mother. I could still break the generational bondage that had tied my family in knots. I could still birth new ideas, one of which you are holding in your hands right now.

It was not until many years later that I understood some of the distorted thinking that affected the Sassytails chapter of my life. It started with good intentions, as so many things in life do. Now that I understand energy and intention, I see it more clearly. The intention behind Sassytails was *desperation*. I was trying to prove myself to the world. I was fighting everyone and everything. The good I was hoping to spread was overshadowed by the fear deep inside. The change I was trying to make was overshadowed by my inability to trust my own decisions. The genuine love I had for inspiring young girls was overshadowed by the lack of love I had for myself. In a nutshell, I was attempting to break free from the Narrative—the twenty-first-century variation of what *The Feminine Mystique* labeled "that which has no name" decades ago.

This path led me to the place where I finally love myself enough—as much as I love my daughter. It is a wonderful place to be.

My life path gave me an opportunity to unplug from the Narrative. Although I didn't know it at the time, when I started investing energy into creating my story, I set aside much of what I was taught from his-story. I started from a blank page. Ten years later, here I am.

The defining difference in the gift you now hold in your hands versus the experience of Sassytails? Everything has shifted. I have the same desire to make a difference, but this time, the intention flows from *love*. Love for myself, love for others, love for my daughter. Love for my sisters around the globe and a heartfelt devotion that transcends time, space, and differences. This time, I have nothing to prove. I am enough, and I know that with every fiber of my being.

The Sassytails experience obliterated everything I once believed, and *that* **has made all the difference.**

THE POWERFUL LIFE
WAITING FOR YOU

When you print the one-page inspiration of the Sisterhood,[148] make a conscious choice to shift your focus to the green zone. What we focus on grows.[149] If you are tempted to focus on the red zone and stop doing these things, then the journey will feel hard. It does not have to be hard. Be ease. Any time you feel powerless, use the guide to find your way. The green zone is where the freedom is. Focus on these empowering mindsets, and the rest will fall away. The Sisterhood has given us a treasure map to freedom.

What does that freedom look like? I was hoping you would ask.

"Intention supported by repetition eventually creates your Truth."

Jabine—My Guardian Angel

CONCLUSION: THIS IS THE LIFE WAITING FOR YOU

When you embrace the truth that I am enough.

You'll realize you no longer have to strive. You no longer have to buy into the mythical mindset that *I have to do more, be more, give more.* You'll realize you don't have to be anything except who you are. Great freedom and peace come with this realization. You will find a lifetime of wisdom in three small words: *I am enough.*

When you live from the mindset of, Here is what I am willing to do.

When you choose to jump into the driver's seat of life, you won't be taking Victimhood or Just along with you for the ride. You'll compassionately understand that many are still blinded by the old mindsets, but you are free. When the world tries to entice you back into the old ways, you'll smile knowingly and hold your ground. And when the chaos begins to overwhelm, you'll know it's time to find a quiet place to recharge. Chatter is not our friend.

You'll calmly draw boundaries, knowing that when you love yourself enough, you will then be able to love and lead others well. You cannot love from a depleted heart. You cannot grow a fertile life if your reservoir is dry. If being selfish is thinking only of yourself and being selfless is thinking only about others, you choose to be *self-full*.[150] And you are the only one who can make that decision. You are responsible for your own life.

When you move forward in confidence.

Living *with* confidence means you're taking something with you, adding more weight to your backpack of life. Living *in* confidence means there's an essence within you that radiates from the inside out. And such *confidence inside* allows you to do many things:

- Realize that it will take time for others to understand and accept your new perspective.

- Take responsibility for how you might have unknowingly trained others to treat you.

- Make your own choices with understanding, conviction, and compassion, knowing that when you make a choice to better your life, it will ultimately better the lives of others.

When you no longer have to consciously "rewrite the Narrative."

It is now woven into your DNA of thought. You've stepped out of the cage you placed yourself in, and now the world is full of possibilities. Whenever the red zone of one of the sisters surprisingly shows up or the world throws a curveball, you respond and rebound quickly. A long time ago, you made the choice to befriend victory over Victimhood.

When you truly believe there is enough for me and you.

You take pride in believing you are the right one for the opportunity. You take more risks. You go after stretch assignments. That job you once thought was out of reach? Now you apply for it—or perhaps create the one that does not yet exist. Or you run for the elected position.

Understanding that there's always risk when you reach, you still go after new opportunities, and if things don't turn out as you hoped, you can accept it. You don't label yourself a failure; instead, you think "not this time." If you know deep down you did your best, then you rest in knowing there is another path. If truthful consideration reveals that you did not, you commit to do the work to move in that direction.

You no longer have to tear others down—men or women—because you know they can succeed *and* you can succeed. We all have different gifts to bring to the world. You choose to be ready for the next opportunity. You don't waste precious time allowing Judgment to do her thing. Instead, you invest your energy into building others up. You choose to *detach from the drama* to which the world is addicted.

When you own and articulate your value.

When this happens, it radiates like a light shining from the inside out. You no longer apologize for standing up for yourself. You stand in your truth—*calmly confident, calmly passionate.* When anyone tries to diminish your influence, you now see the Narrative for what it is—and no longer give it power.

Places or people that cannot or do not appreciate you are slowly carved out of your life. If others don't embrace your personal power, they miss out, but you spend less emotional bandwidth reflecting on it now. You're busy moving forward with a reenergized life, taking delight in new opportunities. You are busy creating a life of choice.

When you fully embrace that your power is much needed in the world.

The time and energy once spent tearing others—or yourself—down is now invested in moving forward. You realize that the ROI of time, energy, and emotions is best spent using your power for good, not to harm. Understanding your emotional bandwidth, you invest your energy wisely. The story is no longer only about you; your sisters are always in the back of your mind.

You no longer depend on approval from others to determine your self-worth or listen to those who try to tear you down. They are living in their own powerless world of Victimhood; you see this clearly now. There is no going back. Instead of striving and proving, you walk away *calmly confident, calmly passionate.* You use the love you have for others to propel you forward, knowing it will fuel a love of self.

You find your dharma. You learn why you are here. You tap into the intuitive intelligence you've had all along but were taught to ignore. You become friends with your Truth. The strength you now have radiates from the inside out, and people cannot help but notice and follow.

You discover the power within, freeing the strength of the lion. When *this* is the life you are living from the inside out, everything shifts. For you. For me. Individually and collectively. Deep down, you know the Truth. Deep down, your soul speaks. "It's time."

"It has been there all along," the Sisterhood whispers. "It is done. It is done. It is done."

#LegacyofLove

Want to be part of the journey and spread the powerful messages in this book? Go to YourLionInside.com to learn about hosting a book club.[151]

TO LEARN MORE ABOUT WAYS OTHER WOMEN HAVE REWRITTEN THE NARRATIVE IN THEIR LIVES, CHECK OUT THE POWERFUL STORIES BELOW AT

WWW.KIMBERLYFAITH.COM/ DOWNLOADS/#INSPIRATION

- *Scenario #1*
  To Unapologetically Be Myself:
  Wisdom from a Latina Sister with
  Susana Leyva[152] and inspired by
  Mellody Hobson[153]

- *Scenario #2*
  The Myth of Ageism with Vivian

- *Scenario #3*
  Opening Commentary for a
  Conference with Sara Kwan[154]

- *Scenario #4*
  Wisdom from a Sister in the Largest
  Fraternity in the World—the Military
  with Kathy Knapp[155]

- *Scenario #5*
  For Our Sisters in Hollywood
  and Entertainment with Reese
  Witherspoon[156]

  I would love to hear your story about
  rewriting the Narrative in your world.

  Email me at

  Kim@KimberlyFaith.com.
  https://www.yourlioninside.com/

Pause - Reflect - Choose

ABOUT THE AUTHOR

Kimberly "Kim" Faith has had the privilege to train, coach, and inspire over thirty thousand leaders from thirty-three countries, spanning twenty-four industries, from companies such as Amazon, American Airlines, BMW, Capgemini, DELL, GE, HCA, Microsoft, Nielsen, and Target. In addition to working on licensing deals with Warner Brothers and Disney through the Sassytails experience, she has led workshops in Brazil, Canada, Dubai, France, Italy, Singapore, Switzerland, and the United States.

Influenced early in her career by the discipline of systems thinking, Kim's work in the field was included in Dr. Peter Senge's *The Fifth Discipline Fieldbook*.[157] Her executive coaching experience led to the development of Breakthru-Branding.com/Career, an online course that inspires professionals to jump into the driver's seat of their careers. To join the online course experience, use the code CORPORATE for a significant discount. Kim is committed to supporting the movement to increase pay equity and elevate the power of choice for all women.

She has been featured in Women's Entrepreneurship, Ladies Who Launch, *The Wall Street Journal,* and *Women's World.* She coauthored her first book, *Unleash Your BS (Best Self),* in 2015. Kim has plans to coauthor another book, with fellow systems thinking expert Linda Dolny, to be released in 2020. It is titled *An Almost True Story: A Miracle of Change* and is designed for both male and female audiences.

Be on the lookout for an exciting new online experience Kim will be launching in 2020 called *Intuitive Intelligence.* This experience will inspire millions of women to embrace their intuitive knowing as their guiding compass. The experience will take you step by step through a gateway, opening a portal into new possibilities—individually and collectively. You will be inspired to tune in to your inner-net versus the internet. Coming soon at MyIntuitiveIntelligence.com.

In February 2016, Kim was chosen as a winner[158] of personal coaching by Cheryl Richardson, *New York Times* best-selling author, and Reid Tracy, CEO and president of Hay House Publishing. Hay House is responsible for authors and teachers like Louise Hay, Wayne Dyer, Suze Orman, Gabrielle Bernstein, and Brendon Bruchard.

"The essence of this book is to magnify HOPE—harnessing our power every day—and to ignite what has been dormant within. I am on a quest to inspire people—and enterprises—to find where they soulfully belong and make their unique contribution to the matrix of life," Kim shares.

"May we encourage those above us, motivate those beside us, and leave a legacy of empowerment for all of those coming after us."

ACKNOWLEDGMENTS

A MESSAGE TO MY SWEET SISTERS

To my sisters in Asia—You are a treasure to behold. Wise. Breathtaking in your purity of soul and purpose. It is my heartfelt wish that the veil of illusion will fall away. Claim the powerful gifts you have been given.

To my sisters in India—Your strength is deep and wide, yet even you may not see the important role you play in this narrative called *being a woman*. Thank you for your steadfastness and strength. Rest in knowing that your steps to break down barriers and forge new paths are not futile. The results are powerful—like a mountain. We can't always see the growth with eyes wide open, yet one day it will appear. Majestic. Tall. Proud.

To my sisters in the UK—Such a breath of fresh air you are! News always sounds better when it comes from you. Nothing like a bloody mess to get things moving, right? Keep your energy, spread it far and wide. Many are in need of a dose of your spirit and feistiness.

To my sisters in Europe—Your ability to move among so many cultures is something we can all learn from. There is no one way to define you, but you don't mind—you prefer it that way. Your global perspective gives you a unique lens through which to see the world. You inspire us to see life as a kaleidoscope—embracing our differences, admiring the beauty, and creating a tapestry of talent.

To my Latina sisters—Your zest for life brings strength and beauty to a world in desperate need of kindness. Your ability to love from a full heart has the power to change the world. Your perseverance is unwavering; your dedication is compelling. May we drink in the magic that is *you*, inspiring us to change the drumbeat of the world one human being at a time.

To my sisters in the Middle East—So many degrees of dizzying expectations threaten to hide the light within. You walk the line, acknowledging all that is steeped in tradition while figuring out the heart's calling to be who you are. Glorious strength. Steadfast courage. Know that we see the treasure you are.

To my sisters in America—You inspire the world with your unwavering dedication, your fearlessness, and your sense of individualism. Many march feeling like we have miles to go when it comes to equality. It was truly a revelation when I realized that in the United States, we are running a sprint compared to our sisters in other countries. They have run three marathons just to arrive where we stand today.

To my sisters I have not yet met—Our paths are destined to cross—somehow, someday. I look forward with great anticipation for that day to arrive. Know that your spirit has been in my heart as the words have poured onto these pages.

The truth is, we are sisters. When you look past the language barriers, past the traditions, past the religious beliefs, past the cultural differences, past the expectations placed upon our shoulders, we are all the same.

Jewels of all colors, shapes, and sizes. Each serving a purpose tied to the collective whole. Each one designed to shine brilliantly.

One last thought, my sisters. Do not be surprised by the pushback you receive—individually and collectively. As we each chip away at the Narrative and it grows smaller, fear will grow. This is a temporary reaction. Our collective empowerment will render some institutions and systems irrelevant. They will fight to stay alive. Stay the course, and draw close to the Sisterhood for strength. It is all part of the dance of change.

To learn more about the system, go to https://epicenterofchange.com/.

My beloved Peter—In the heart space that is you, you gave me a safe place to blossom. I will forever be grateful. Your legacy lives on.

Heather—You are the light of my life. You have inspired me in so many ways. Thank you for leading me to the best version of myself.

Awareness CURRENT MENTAL MODEL —your beliefs, mindsets

Choice A NEW MENTAL MODEL ...this is the first step

Freedom YOUR DESIRED FUTURE ...a BIG shift in the mental model

Mental models are the "lens" through which we see the world. The beliefs are not good or bad—they simply are. The danger is when we unconsciously operate from those beliefs. We have the power to CHOOSE!

	CURRENT MENTAL MODEL	A NEW MENTAL MODEL	YOUR DESIRED FUTURE
KARI	THE KARI STORY: I expect perfection	I believe DONE is better than perfect	I AM enough
RANEE	THE RANEE STORY: I have to meet all demands	I CAN say no	Here is what I am willing to do
GABRIELLA	THE GABRIELLA STORY: I need permission/approval	I TRUST my own decisions	I can move forward in confidence
DARSHA	THE DARSHA STORY: I should accept what is said (or done)	I CAN pause, reflect and choose	I choose to rewrite the narrative
AVALENE	THE AVALENE STORY: I'm not qualified enough	I AM the right one for the opportunity	There is enough for me AND you
JALILA	THE JALILA STORY: If I work hard enough, I will be rewarded	I can advocate and CARE for myself	I own and articulate my value
NIKKI	THE NIKKI STORY: I'm okay in the background	I AM powerful and that's okay	My power is MUCH needed in this world

Stop allowing these mindsets to stand in the way. ...... *Slowly allow your light to shine brighter...* ...... *Go forward and unleash your best self!*

VICTIMHOOD: Powerless: Defensive .... Offensive: Powerful: VICTORY

© KimberlyFaith 2017 | yourLIONinside.com

PODCAST

For more information about Kimberly Faith, please visit:

- YourLionInside.com

- KimberlyFaith.com

- MyIntuitiveIntelligence.com

You can also reach Kim via the following:

linkedin.com/in/kimberlyfaith

Twitter: @IamKimFaith

youtube.com/c/KimberlyFaithInspires

instagram.com/KimberlyFaithInspires

pinterest.com/KimberlyFaithInspires/

Facebook: Kimberly Faith—Author

For more information on rewriting the narrative, check out:

TheSisterhoodReportPodcast.com
EpicenterofChange.com

For media interviews, workshops, and keynote inquires,
contact Kim@KimberlyFaith.com.

Endnotes

1   Leigh A. Caldwell, "Face the Facts: A Fact Check on Gas Prices," *CBS News*, March 21, 2012, https://www.cbsnews.com/news/face-the-facts-a-fact-check-on-gas-prices/. Gas was over four dollars a gallon.

2   Peter M. Senge, *The Fifth Discipline: The Art and Practice of the Learning Organization* (New York: Doubleday/Currency, 2006), 40.

3   Paul Selig, *The Mastery Trilogy: Books 1–3* (TarcherPerigee, 2016, 2017, 2018).

4   "About International Women's Day," International Women's Day, accessed September 12, 2019, http://www.internationalwomensday.com/About.

5   Achievements of Susan B. Anthony. "Her Life," The National Susan B. Anthony Museum & House, accessed September 12, 2019, https://susanb.org/her-life/; Penny Colman, Elizabeth Cady Stanton and Susan B. Anthony: A Friendship That Changed the World (New York: Henry Holt and Company, 2013); Ruth Rosen, The World Split Open: How the Modern Women's Movement Changed America (New York: Penguin Books, 2000).

6   19th amendment. "Suffragist," The National Susan B. Anthony Museum & House, accessed September 12, 2019, https://susanb.org/suffragist/.

7   Stephen Cope, *The Great Work of Your Life: A Guide for the Journey to Your True Calling* (New York: Bantam Books, 2012).

8   Anirudh, "10 Major Accomplishments of Susan B Anthony," Learnodo Newtonic, October 5, 2015, https://

learnodo-newtonic.com/susan-b-anthony-accomplishments. Susan B. Anthony did have a message that day.

9   Cope, 91.

10   Cope, 97.

11   "Stanton/Anthony Friendship," Susan B. Anthony Center, University of Rochester, accessed September 12, 2019,   http://www.rochester.edu/sba/suffrage-history/ stantonanthony-friendship/.

12   My Hero, "Susan B. Anthony," Amanda from San Diego, accessed September 13, 2019, https://myhero. com/S_Anthony_dnhs_kt_US_2014_ul.

13   Cope, 97–98.

14   Cope, 98.

15   Madora Kibbe, "The Pot Roast Principle," *Psychology Today*, February 8, 2014, https://www.psychologytoday.com/ blog/thinking-makes-it-so/201402/the-pot-roast-principle. I have shared this story for over twenty years. I have never been able to find the origin of the story, but it is used routinely.

16   Sheryl Sandberg, *Lean In: Women, Work, and the Will to Lead* (New York: Alfred A. Knopf, 2013).

17   Lean In, https://leanin.org/.

18   Julie Weeks, "Lean In Sparks Push Back," The Story Exchange, April 4, 2013, https://thestoryexchange.org/ lean-sparks-push/.

19   Rachel Thomas, "Having Six Women Running for President Changes Everything," *Marie Claire*, July 30, 2019,   https://www.marieclaire.com/politics/a28552462/ women-2020-debate-only-experience/.

20 Heather Caygle, "Record-Breaking Number of Women Run for Office," *Politico*, March 8, 2018, https://www.politico.com/story/2018/03/08women-rule-midterms-443267.

21 "Danielle Kurtzleben, "More Than Twice as Many Women Are Running for Congress in 2018 Compared with 2016," *NPR Morning Edition*, February 20, 2018, https://www.npr.org/2018/02/20/585542531/more-than-twice-as-many-women-are-running-for-congress-in-2018-com-pared-to-2016?t=1557991623990.

22 Senge, *The Fifth Discipline*, 89. The Narrative is derived from the idea that the system has a life of its own.

23 Caryl Rivers and Rosalind C. Barnett, "8 Big Problems for Women in the Workplace," *Chicago Tribune*, May 18, 2016, http://www.chicagotribune.com/news/opinion/commentary/ct-women-pay-gap-workplace-equal-ity-perspec-0519-jm-20160518-story.html.

24 Peter M. Senge, *The Dance of Change: The Challenges to Sustaining Momentum in a Learning Organization* (New York: Doubleday, 1999).

25 "Rent the Runway CEO: Building a Closet in the Cloud," July 1, 2018, on *Boss Files with Poppy Harlow*, produced by Haley Draznin, 57 minutes, https://podcasts.apple.com/us/podcast/rent-the-runway-ceo-building-a-closet-in-the-cloud/id1201282406?i=1000415062242.

26 J. Clara Chan, "Elizabeth Warren: Why Run for President Just to Say 'What We Really Can't Do and Shouldn't

Fight For'?" *The Wrap*, July 30, 2019, https://www.thewrap.com/elizabeth-warren-why-run-for-president-just-to-say-what-we-really-cant-do-and-shouldnt-fight-for/.

27 Jennifer Y. Hyman, "Treating Workers Fairly at Rent the Runway," *New York Times*, May 6, 2018.

28 Gregg Braden, "Look for Signs in Nature," Nature's Keys to the Universe blog, 2009, https://www.greggbraden.com/blog/look-signs-nature/.

29 Libby Birk, "Real Tips from Women Who Have Lost 30 Pounds Or More," Popculture, September 6, 2019, http://womanista.com/wellness/2016/10/07/real-tips-from-women-who-have-lost-30-pounds-or-more/.

30 Epicenter of Change, https://epicenterofchange.com/.

31 Selig, *The Book of Knowing and Worth* (New York: Jeremy P. Tarcher/Penguin, 2013), 77.

32 Women in the Workplace Study, McKinsey & Company and Lean In, https://womenintheworkplace.com/.

33 Melinda Gates, *The Moment of Lift: How Empowering Women Changes the World* (New York: Flatiron Books, 2019).

34 "Unintended Consequences," Future Learn, accessed September 13, 2019, https://www.futurelearn.com/courses/systems-thinking-complexity/0/steps/20396.

35 Daniel Kim, "Shifting the Burden: The 'Helen Keller' Loops," The Systems Thinker, accessed September 13, 2019, https://thesystemsthinker.com/shifting-the-burden-the-helen-keller-loops/.

36 "Timelines of Women's Suffrage Granted," The Nelle McClung Foundation, accessed September 12, 2019, https://www.ournellie.com/learn/womens-suffrage/political-equality-timeline/.

37 Kimberly Faith, "Rose Defonzo 100th Birthday Montage 1," YouTube video, February 18, 2016, https://www.youtube.com/watch?v=ep3Vrw_TwNo&feature=youtu.be.

38 Women's March, accessed September 12, 2019, https://www.womensmarch.com/.

39 International Women's Day, accessed September 12, 2019, https://www.internationalwomensday.com/.

40 James Barron, "Wounded by 'Fearless Girl,' Creator of 'Charging Bull' Wants Her to Move," New York Times, April 12, 2017, https://www.nytimes.com/2017/04/12/nyregion/charging-bull-sculpture-wall-street-fearless-girl.html.

41 Angela Russell, "Author: Hillary Clinton's Loss Was 'Greatest Gift to Women's Movement," King 5 News, July 18, 2019, https://www.king5.com/article/news/local/take-5/author-hillary-clintons-loss-was-greatest-gift-to-womens-movement/281-fab5bf7a-ecca-44ef-a8ee-0859132c871b.

42 Jodi Kantor and Megan Twohey, "Harvey Weinstein Paid Off Sexual Harassment Accusers for Decades," New York Times, October 5, 2017, https://www.nytimes.com/2017/10/05/us/harvey-weinstein-harassment-allega-tions.html.

43 "The Jeffrey Epstein Scandal," *The Cut*, last updated August 21, 2019, https://www.thecut.com/tags/the-jeffrey-epstein-scandal.

44 James Walker, "#HerStory: Twitter Launches Campaign Highlighting Work of Female Journalists in US," *PressGazette*, May 3, 2019, https://www.pressgazette.co.uk/hcrstory-twitter-launches-campaign-highlighting-work-of-female-journalists-in-us/.

45 Alanna Vagianos, "The 'Me Too' Campaign Was Created by a Black Woman 10 Years Ago," *HuffPost*, October 17, 2017, https://www.huffpost.com/entry/the-me-too-campaign-was-created-by-a-black-woman-10-years-ago_n_5 9e61a7fe4b02a215b336fee.

46 Pier Luigi Luisi, "Systems Thinking and Its Implications: The Principle of Interdependence," *Wall Street International*, January 29, 2016, https://wsimag.com/science-and-technology/19190-systems-thinking-and-its-implications.

47 "Who Was Ella Baker?" Ella Baker Center for Human Rights, accessed September 12, 2019, https://ella-bakercenter.org/about/who-was-ella-baker.

48 Debra Michals, ed., "Sojourner Truth," National Women's History Museum, 2015, https://www.womenshis-tory.org/education-resources/biographies/sojourner-truth.

49 The Editors of Encyclopaedia Britannica, "Alice Walker," *Britannica*, https://www.britannica.com/biography/Alice-Walker.

50 Colman, 92–93.

51 Colman, 22.

52   Daniel Christian Wahl, "Donella Meadows Recommendations for How to Dance with and Intervene in Systems," Hacker Noon, October 3, 2017, https://hackernoon.com/donella-meadows-recommendations-for-how-to-dance-with-and-intervene-in-systems-92ace21743fb.

53   Senge, *The Fifth Discipline*, 101.

54   Dr. Matthew Price, LinkedIn profile, https://www.linkedin.com/in/matthewpricephd/.

55   Gigi DeVault, "What Is Sentiment Analysis?" The Balance, April 25, 2018, https://www.thebalancesmb.com/what-is-sentiment-analysis-2296941.

56   Micah Brown, "Micah Brown Articles," Centiment Blog, accessed December 23, 2017, https://centiment.io/beta/blog/author/micah-brown-ceo/. All screenshots of data were created using the software from Centiment at various times throughout 2017.

57   Centiment, "Centiment Demo Day," Vimeo video, June 29, 2017, https://vimeo.com/223705717.

58   Linda and Charlie Bloom, "The Bandwagon Effect," *Psychology Today*, August 11, 2017, https://www.psychologytoday.com/blog/stronger-the-broken-places/201708/the-bandwagon-effect.

59   "Availability Heuristic," iResearchNet.com, accessed September 12, 2019, http://psychology.iresearchnet.com/social-psychology/social-cognition/availability-heuristic/.

60   Ryan McElhany, "The Effects of Anchoring Bias on Human Behavior," SAGU ThoughtHub,

May 23, 2016, https://www.sagu.edu/thoughthub/the-affects-of-anchoring-bias-on-human-behavior.

61 Ashley E. Martin and Katherine W. Phillips, "What 'Blindness' to Gender Differences Helps Women See and Do: Implications for Confidence, Agency, and Action in Male-Dominated Environments," *Organizational Behavior and Human Decision Processes* 142 (September 2017): 28–44, https://doi.org/10.1016/j.obhdp.2017.07.004.

62 Andrea C. Vial and Jaime L. Napier, "High Power Mindsets Reduce Gender Identification and Benevolent Sexism among Women (But Not Men)," *Journal of Experimental Social Psychology* 68 (January 2017): 162–70, https://doi.org/10.1016/j.jesp.2016.06.012.

63 Souha R. Ezzedeen, "The Portrayal of Professional and Managerial Women in North American Films: Good News or Bad News for Your Executive Pipeline?" *Organizational Dynamics* 42, no. 4 (October–December 2013): 248–56, https://doi.org/10.1016/j.orgdyn.2013.07.002.

64 "The Glass Ceiling," *The Economist*, May 5, 2009, http://www.economist.com/node/13604240.

65 Meadows, 159.

66 Deborah A. Bolnick et al., "The Science and Business of Genetic Ancestry Testing," *Science* 318, no. 5849 (October 19, 2007): 399–400, https://doi.org/10.1126/science.1150098.

67 Gina Kolata, "With a Simple DNA Test, Family Histories Are Rewritten," *New York Times*, August 28, 2017,

https://www.nytimes.com/2017/08/28/science/dna-tests-ancestry.html.

68 "Using DNA to Solve Crimes," US Department of Justice Archives, accessed September 12, 2019, https://www.justice.gov/archives/ag/advancing-justice-through-dna-technology-using-dna-solve-crimes.

69 Dan Baker and Cameron Stauth, *What Happy People Know: How the New Science of Happiness Can Change Your Life for the Better* (Rodale, 2003), 135.

70 India.Arie, *Strength, Courage & Wisdom*, Universal Import, 2002, compact disc; Aretha Franklin, *A Rose Is Still a Rose*, Arista, 1998, compact disc; "Q.U.E.E.N.," featuring Erykah Badu, track 3 on Janelle Monáe, *The Electric Lady*, Wondaland Arts Society, 2013, compact disc; "Beautiful," track 11 on Christina Aguilera, *Stripped*, RCA, 2003, compact disc; Lady Gaga, *Born This Way*, Interscope Records, 2011, compact disc. I asked for suggestions from many colleagues when it came to gathering songs, books, movies, and true stories to inspire. There are many more examples to be added in the future. This list is simply to get you started and are recommendations only. KF Enterprises Inc., or Kimberly Faith, has no liability for content in third-party materials or links.

71 Brené Brown, *The Gifts of Imperfection: Let Go of Who You Think You're Supposed to Be and Embrace Who You Are* (Center City, MN: Hazelden Publishing, 2010); Brown, *Dare to Lead: Brave Work. Tough Conversations. Whole Hearts* (New York: Random House, 2018); *Moana*, directed by Ron

Clements and John Musker, (United States: Walt Disney Pictures, 2016); Cheryl Strayed, *Wild: From Lost to Found on the Pacific Crest Trail* (New York: Vintage Books, 2012).

72 Great Big Story, "Untangling the Roots of Dominican Hair," YouTube video, April 3, 2017, https://www.youtube.com/watch?v=XwtnFGB9c_c; The Stay At Home Chef, "Why My Gray Hairs Make Me Happy," YouTube video, November 22, 2016, https://www.youtube.com/watch?v=aFk9L3nhS0Q&feat re=youtu.be; Goalcast, "Mel Robbins—Outsmart Your Brain," video, July 23, 2017, https://www.goalcast.com/2017/07/24/mel-robbins-felt-like-a-complete-failure/; OWN, "SuperSoul Short: Kidada Jones, School of Awake," YouTube video, October 25, 2017, https://www.youtube.com/watch?v=16f_x4Qhycw&feature=youtu.be.

73 Hoffman, "Feelings List," Hoffman Institute Foundation, March 15, 2013, https://www.hoffmaninstitute.org/wp-content/uploads/Practices-FeelingsSensations.pdf.

74 "Defying Gravity," track 11 on Kristin Chenoweth and Idina Menzel, *Wicked*, Verve, 2003, compact disc; "No," track 3 on Meghan Trainor, *Thank You*, Epic, 2016, compact disc; "Golden," track 3 on Jill Scott, *Beautifully Human: Words and Sounds Vol. 2*, Hidden Beach Records, 2015, compact disc; "You Don't Own Me," track 7 on Lesley Gore, *Lesley Gore Sings of Mixed-Up Hearts*, Mercury Records, 1963, compact disc.

75 *The Devil Wears Prada*, directed by David Frankel, (United States: Fox 2000 Pictures and Dune Entertainment,

2006); *Mona Lisa Smile*, directed by Mike Newell, (United States: Revolution Studios and Red Om Films Productions, 2003); *Norma Rae*, directed by Martin Ritt (United States: 20th Century Fox, 1979).

76 CBS Sunday Morning, "Q&A: Melinda Gates," YouTube video, March 5, 2017, https://www.youtube. com/watch?v=yu45Ct-dzoM; Great Big Story, "I Don't Need Her Permission": Art as a Weapon for Women, video, accessed September 12, 2019, http://www.great-bigstory.com/stories/instigators-michelle-hartney-s-quest-to-give-women-a-choice; 99U, *Liz Jackson: Designing for Inclusivity*, video, 2017, http://99u.com/videos/55965/liz-jackson-designing-for-inclusivity.

77 "Freedom," featuring Kendrick Lamar, track 10 on Beyoncé, *Lemonade*, Parkwood Entertainment/Columbia, 2016, compact disc; Demi Lovato, *Confident*, Hollywood Records, 2015, compact disc; "What Doesn't Kill You (Stronger)," track 2 on Kelly Clarkson, *Stronger*, RCA Records Label, 2011, compact disc; "Greatest Love of All," track 9 on Whitney Houston, *Whitney Houston*, Arista, 1985, compact disc; "Grateful," track 13 on Rita Ora, *Beyond the Lights* soundtrack, Relativity Music, 2014, compact disc.

78 *Erin Brockovich*, directed by Steven Soderbergh (United States: Jersey Films, 2000); *Black*, directed by Sanjay Leela Bhansali (India: Applause Entertainment and SLB Films, 2005); *G.I. Jane*, directed by Ridley Scott (United States: Buena Vista Pictures, 1997).

79 Great Big Story, "Nigeria's First Female Car Mechanic Is Changing the World," video, 2016, http://www.greatbig-story.com/stories/meet-nigeria-s-first-female-car-mechanic; Manal al-Sharif, "A Saudi Woman Who Dared to Drive," TEDGlobal 2013, video, June 2013, https://www.ted.com/talks/manal_al_sharif_a_saudi_woman_who_dared_to_drive; Atika Shubert and Nadine Schmidt, "The Septuage-narian Fighting Hate with a Spray Can," *CNN*, December 17, 2016, http://edition.cnn.com/2016/12/17/europe/irmela-schramm-fights-berlin-street-art-racism/index.html.

80 "The Self-Fulfilling Prophecy," University Discover-ies, accessed September 12, 2019, http://university-discover-ies.com/the-self-fulfilling-prophecy.

81 "Fighter," track 4 on Christina Aguilera, *Stripped*, RCA Records, 2002, compact disc; "Feeling Good," track 3 on Nina Simone, *The Very Best of Nina Simone*, Sony BMG, 2006, compact disc; "Shake It Off," track 6 on Taylor Swift, *1989*, Big Machine Records and Republic Records, 2014, compact disc; "Roar," track 1 on Katy Perry, *Prism*, Capitol Records, 2013, compact disc; "Own It," track 12 on The Black Eyed Peas, *The Beginning*, Interscope, 2010, compact disc.

82 Glennon Doyle, Untamed (Random House, 2020).

83 Marianne Williamson, A Politics of Love (Harper-Collins, 2019).

84 *Hidden Figures*, directed by Theodore Melfi (United States: 20th Century Fox, 2016); *The Help*, directed by Tate Taylor (United States, India, United Arab Emirates: Walt

Disney Studios Motion Pictures, 2011); Trina Paulus, *Hope for the Flowers* (Mahwah, New Jersey: Paulist Press, 2014; Rachel Denhollander, *What Is a Girl Worth?: My Story of Breaking the Silence and Exposing the Truth about Larry Nassar and USA Gymnastics* (Carol Stream: Ill: Tyndale Momentum, 2019.

85 Great Big Story, "Creating Community with Spain's All-Female Cricket Team," video, 2017, https://www.greatbigstory.com/stories/creating-community-with-spain-s-all-female-cricket-team; Great Big Story, "Body-building at 80," video, 2017, https://www.greatbigstory.com/stories/fitness-goals-bodybuilding-at-80-years-old; BuzzFeed, "Brave And Tragic: A Story Of Being One Of The Mengele Twins In The Holocaust," Facebook video, September 26, 2017, https://www.facebook.com/BuzzFeed/videos/10156791799070329/; Great Big Story, "How a News Anchor Broke the Mold and Found Her Voice," video, accessed September 13, 2019, https://www.greatbigstory.com/stories/shine-anchor-beauty; Great Big Story, "Blowing Up Stereotypes with a Chemistry Professor," video, accessed September 13, 2019, https://www.greatbigstory.com/stories/blowing-up-stereotypes-with-a-chemistry-professor.

86 "Salute, track 1 on Little Mix, *Salute*, Syco, 2013, compact disc; "I'm Coming Out," track 4 on Diana Ross, *Diana*, Motown, 1980, compact disc; "I'm Every Woman," track 3 on Whitney Houston, *The Bodyguard*, Arista, 1992, compact disc; "You Will (The OWN Song)," MP3 audio,

Jennifer Hudson and Jennifer Nettles, RCA Records Label, 2015.

87 *Mean Girls*, directed by Mark Waters (United States: Paramount Pictures, 2004); Sue Monk Kidd, *The Secret Life of Bees* (New York: Penguin Books, 2003); *A League of Their Own*, directed by Penny Marshall (United States: Columbia Pictures, 1992).

88 Great Big Story, "Inside Japan's Only All-Female Sushi House," video, 2017, https://www.greatbigstory.com/stories/all-female-sushi-house; Howard Schultz and Rajiv Chandrasekaran, "Upstanders: A Racists Rehabilitation," Starbucks Stories & News, October 18, 2017, https://news.starbucks.com/news/upstanders-a-racists-rehabilitation; Great Big Story, "Instigators: The Midwife of La Cienega Boulevard," video, 2015, https://www.greatbigstory.com/stories/instigators-the-midwife-of-la-cienega-boulevard.

89 Mika Brzezinski, *Knowing Your Value: Women, Money, and Getting What You're Worth* (New York: Weinstein Books, 2011).

90 Meadows, 89; Senge, *The Fifth Discipline*, 52.

91 "Independent Women Part 1," track 1 on Destiny's Child, *Survivor*, Columbia, 2001, compact disc; "Respect," track 1 on Aretha Franklin, *I Never Loved a Man the Way I Love You*, Atlantic, 1967, compact disc; "Just Fine," track 3 on Mary J. Blige, *Growing Pains*, Geffen, 2007, compact disc; Ani DiFranco, *Not a Pretty Girl*, Righteous Babe Records, 2017, compact disc.

92 *Legally Blonde*, directed by Robert Luketic (United States: MGM Distribution Co., 2001); Malala Yousafzai, *I Am Malala: The Girl Who Stood Up for Education and Was Shot by the Taliban* (London: Weidenfeld & Nicholson, 2013).

93 Rana El Kaliouby, PHD, and Carol Colman, Girl Decoded (Penguin RandomHouse, 2020).

94 Sophia Amoruso, #GIRLBOSS (Portfolio, 2015).

95 Great Big Story, "Claressa: Fighting to Stay on Top," video, 2016, https://www.greatbigstory.com/stories/claressa#; Great Big Story, "Breaking Silicon Valley's Glass Ceiling," video, accessed September 13, 2019, https://www.greatbigstory.com/stories/guest-editor-diversity-advocate.

96 Kimberly Faith, "Nikki's Story on Personal Branding & Confidence," YouTube video, April 26, 2017, https://www.youtube.com/watch?v=j8_OgjJ4iA4&feature=youtu.be.

97 "This Is for My Girls," Chloe & Halle, Jadagrace, Janelle Monáe, Kelly Clarkson, Kelly Rowland, Lea Michele, Missy Elliott, and Zendaya, Motown Records, 2016, compact disc; "Run the World (Girls)," track 12 on Beyoncé, *4*, Columbia, 2011, compact disc; "Fight Song," track 1 on Rachel Platten, *Fight Song*, Columbia, 2015, compact disc; "Unwritten," track 4 on Natasha Bedingfield, *Unwritten*, Phonogenic and Epic, 2004, compact disc; "Superwoman," track 3 on Alicia Keys, *As I Am*, J Records, 2007, compact disc.

98 *Wonder Woman*, directed by Patty Jenkins (United States: Warner Bros. Pictures, 2017); *The Post*, directed by Steven Spielberg, (United States: 20th Century Fox and Universal Pictures, 2017); *The Hunger Games*, directed by Gary Ross (United States: Lionsgate Films, 2012); *On the Basis of Sex*, directed by Mimi Leder (United States: Focus Features, 2018); *Coco before Chanel*, directed by Anne Fontaine (France and Belgium: Warner Bros. Pictures, 2009); Melinda Gates, *The Moment of Lift: How Empowering Women Changes the World* (New York: Flatiron Books, 2019); Shannon Watts, *Fight Like a Mother: How a Grassroots Movement Took on the Gun Lobby and Why Women Will Change the World* (New York: HarperCollins Publishers, 2019); Joan Chittister, *The Time Is Now: A Call to Uncommon Courage* (New York: Convergent Books, 2019); Charlotte S. Waisman and Jill S. Tietjen, *Her Story: A Timeline of the Women Who Changed America* (New York: HarperCollins Publishers, 2013).

99 Great Big Story, "A Field Between: Former CIA Operative Risks Life to Promote Peace, video, 2017, https://www.greatbigstory.com/stories/a-field-between-a-really-great-big-story?playall=531; Fox Family Entertainment, "The Greatest Showman: 'This Is Me' with Keala Settle," YouTube video, December 24, 2017. https://www.youtube.com/watch?v=XLFEvHWD_NE&feature=youtu.be; Great Big Story, "Taking Back the Neighborhood with an Army of Moms," video, 2016, https://www.greatbigstory.com/stories/the-army-of-moms-standing-up-to-gun-violence; Great Big Story, "A Cafe Run by Heroes," video, 2016, https://www.

greatbigstory.com/stories/a-cafe-run-by-heroes; Great Big Story, "The Women Making History in Georgia's Justice System," video, accessed September 13, 2019, https://www. greatbigstory.com/stories/guest-editor-yvonne-orji-female-court; Great Big Story, "Afghanistan Female Journalists Risk Their Lives to Tell the News," video, September 13, 2019, https://www.greatbigstory.com/stories/femaie-journalist-tv.

100   Kimberly Faith, 2017, https://www.kimber-lyfaith.com/inspiration/.

101   Epicenter of Change, https://epicenterof-change.com/.

102   Wayne W. Dyer, *The Power of Intention*, (Carlsbad, CA: Hay House Inc., 2005).

103   Kim Madden and Heather Madden, "President/Sassy Empress and 8 Yrs. Old, VP of Ideas | Ladies Who Launch," *Ladies Who Launch* (blog), July 30, 2005, http://www.ladieswholaunch.com/magazine/presidentsassy-empress-8-yrs-old-vp-of-ideas/.

104   Eve Gumpel, "Working with My Mom," *Entrepreneur*, May 9, 2008, https://www.entrepreneur.com/article/218041.

105   "Connect ... Your Business to Your Family," Women's Leadership Exchange, accessed September 13, 2019, http://www.womensleadershipexchange.com/index.php?pagename=resourceinfo&resourcekey=380.

106   "Sassy Tails Ties Up Booming Hair Accessory Market," Cision PRWeb, February 16, 2007, https://www.prweb.com/releases/2007/02/prweb505444.htm.

107   Senge, *The Fifth Discipline*, 95; Meadows, 103.

108   Kimberly Amadeo, "2008 Financial Crisis: The Causes and Costs of the Worst Crisis Since the Great Depression," The Balance, May 11, 2019, https://www.thebalance.com/2008-financial-crisis-3305679; Paul Solman, "How the 2008 Financial Crisis Crashed the Economy and Changed the World," *PBS Newshour*, September 13, 2018, https://www.pbs.org/newshour/show/how-the-2008-financial-crisis-crashed-the-economy-and-changed-the-world.

109   Senge, *The Fifth Discipline*, 19.

110   DECA Event Featured in Future CEO Stars, November 2007, 27, http://fcs.entre-ed.org/pdf/november_year_1.pdf.

111   Kimberly Faith, "A Look at a Past Chapter of My Life—Sassytails 9 yr old VP," YouTube video, May 16, 2016, https://www.youtube.com/watch?v=m3jB4h43zS4&feature=youtu.be.

112   Sarah E. Needleman, "Hitched to a Star," *Wall Street Journal*, August 11, 2008, https://www.wsj.com/articles/SB121803434850417023.

113   *The Wizard of Oz*, directed by Victor Fleming (United States: Loew's, 1939).

114   Marianne Williamson, *Tears to Triumph: Spiritual Healing for the Modern Plagues of Anxiety and Depression* (New York: HarperCollins Publishers, 2016), 14, 76, 78, and 111.

115   Stephanie Zacharek, Eliana Dockterman, and Haley Sweetland Edwards, "*Time* Person of the

Year 2017: The Silence Breakers," *Time*, http://time.com/
time-person-of-the-year-2017-silence-breakers/.

116   Joanne Lipman, *That's What She Said: What
Men Need to Know (and Women Need to Tell Them) About
Working Together* (New York: HarperCollins Publishers,
2018).

117   Betty Friedan, *The Feminine Mystique* (New
York: W. W. Norton & Company, 1963).

118   Senge, *The Fifth Discipline*, 195, 360.

119   Leta Hong Fincher, *Betraying Big Brother:
The Feminist Awakening in China* (New York: Verso, 2018).

120   Saadia Zahidi, *Fifty Million Rising: The New
Generation of Working Women Transforming the Muslim World*
(New York: Nation Books, 2018).

121   Meadows, 145.

122   Shannon Watts, *Fight Like a Mother: How a
Grassroots Movement Took on the Gun Lobby and Why Women
Will Change the World* (New York: HarperCollins Publishers,
2019).

123   Hadley Freeman, "How Was Larry Nassar
Able to Abuse So Many Gymnasts for So Long?" *The Guardian*,
January 26, 2018, https://www.theguardian.com/sport/2018/
jan/26/larry-nassar-abuse-gymnasts-scandal-culture.

124   Marian Reda, "Girl Wins First Case
Against Harasser in Upper Egypt," *Egypt Today*, February
23, 2018, https://www.egypttoday.com/Article/2/43616/
Girl-wins-first-case-against-harasser-in-Upper-Egypt.

125   "EBR District Attorney Reports 14 Domestic Violence-Related Homicides in 2017, IRIS Domestic Violence Center, accessed September 12, 2019, http://www.stopdv.org/index.php/statistics/; and https://www.respect.gov.au/wp-content/uploads/2016/06/conversation_guide.pdf.

126   Claire Zillman, "A New Poll on Sexual Harassment Suggests Why 'Me Too' Went So Insanely Viral," *Fortune*, October 17, 2017, http://fortune.com/2017/10/17/me-too-hashtag-sexual-harassment-at-work-stats.

127   "Dating Abuse Statistics," loveisrespect, accessed September 11, 2019, https://www.loveisrespect.org/resources/dating-violence-statistics/.

128   Zoe Zaczek, "More Than One Quarter of Young People Believe It's Okay for a 'Usually Gentle Man to Slap His Girlfriend,'" *Daily Mail Australia*, October 3, 2018, https://www.dailymail.co.uk/news/article-6234163/More-quarter-young-people-believe-okay-drunk-man-slap-girlfriend.html.

129   Helen Hawkes, "Sticks and Stones to Break Mould in Theatre and Homes," *Chinchilla News*, January 23, 2016, https://www.chinchillanews.com.au/news/sticks-and-stones/2906115/.

130   Mark DeWolf, "12 Stats about Working Women," *US Department of Labor Blog*, March 1, 2017, https://blog.dol.gov/2017/03/01/12-stats-about-working-women.

131   Terence P. Jeffrey, "Women Earn 57% of US Bachelor's Degrees—For the 18th

Straight Year," *CNSNews*, June 8, 2018, https://www.cnsnews.com/news/article/terence-p-jeffrey/women-earn-57-us-bachelors-degrees-18th-straight-year.

132   Mark DeWolf, "12 Stats about Working Women," *US Department of Labor Blog*, March 1, 2017, https://blog.dol.gov/2017/03/01/12-stats-about-working-women.

133   Ana Maria Munoz-Boudet and Ana Revenga, "Breaking the STEM Ceiling for Girls," Brookings Institution, March 7, 2017, https://www.brookings.edu/blog/future-development/2017/03/07/breaking-the-stem-ceiling-for-girls.

134   Perri Klass, "Breaking Gender Stereotypes in the Toy Box," *New York Times*, February 5, 2018, https://www.nytimes.com/2018/02/05/well/family/gender-stereo-types-children-toys.html.

135   Elissa Nadworny, "From Poverty to Rocket Scientist to CEO, a Girl Scout's Inspiring Story," *All Things Considered* on *NPR*, September 5, 2018, https://www.npr.org/2018/09/05/644383683/from-poverty-to-rocket-scien-tist-to-ceo-a-girl-scouts-inspiring-story.

136   "42 New Girl Scout Badges to Change the World," *gsblog*, July 16, 2019, https://blog.girlscouts.org/2019/07/big-news-42-new-girl-scout-badges-to.html.

137   Lisa Respers France, "How Jessica Chastain Got Octavia Spencer Five Times the Pay," *CNN*, January 26, 2018, https://www.cnn.com/2018/01/26/entertainment/octavia-spencer-jessica-chastain-pay/index.html.

138   Jackson Katz, *The Macho Paradox: Why Some Men Hurt Women and How All Men Can Help* (Naperville, Illinois: Sourcebooks, 2006).

139   Warren Farrell and John Gray, "The Boy Crisis: Why Our Boys Are Struggling and What We Can Do About It" (Dallas: BenBella Books, 2018).

140   Glennon Doyle, *Love Warrior: A Memoir* (New York: Flatiron Books, 2016).

141   Kaia Ra, *The Sophia Code: A Living Transmission from the Sophia Dragon Tribe*, 2nd ed. (Kaia Ra and Ra-El Publishing, 2016), 45.

142   Matt Price, "Did You Know? Media's Impact on the Narrative of Women," The Sisterhood Report, podcast episode 2, October 28, 2018, https://www.thesisterhoodreportpodcast.com/podcast/episode-2-dr-matt-price/.

143   Paulo Coelho, *The Alchemist* (New York: HarperCollins Publishers, 1998).

144   Robert H. Lustig, *The Hacking of the American Mind: The Science Behind the Corporate Takeover of Our Bodies and Brains* (New York: Avery, 2017).

145   Catherine Price, *How to Break Up with Your Phone: The 30-Day Plan to Take Back Your Life* (New York: Ten Speed Press, 2018).

146   Angela Saini, *Inferior: How Science Got Women Wrong—and the New Research That's Rewriting the Story* (Boston: Beacon Press, 2018).

147   Emily Chang, *Brotopia: Breaking Up the Boys' Club of Silicon Valley* (New York: Portfolio/Penguin, 2019).

148   Kimberly Faith, 2017, https://www.kimberlyfaith.com/inspiration/.

149   Kiran Jawahrani, "Living Your Convictions to the Last Mile: Courageous Conversations," The Sisterhood Report, podcast episode 17, July 9, 2019, https://www.thesisterhoodreportpodcast.com/podcast/episode-17-kiran-jawahrani-global-leader-bold-strategist-mumbai-maharashtra-india/.

150   Carol Mann, Cosmic Cafe, accessed September 12, 2019, http://yourcosmiccafe.com/.

151   *Your Lion Inside* Book Club Outline, PDF,   https://www.kimberlyfaith.com/wp-content/uploads/2018/03/Book-2018_Web-ready.pdf.

152   Susana Leyva, LinkedIn profile, https://www.linkedin.com/in/susana-leyva-58a2b48/

153   Bethany McLean, "Why Sheryl Sandberg, Bill Bradley, and Oprah Love Mellody Hobson," *Vanity Fair*, March 30, 2015, https://www.vanityfair.com/news/2015/03/mellody-hobson-ariel-investments-fighting-stereotype.

154   Sara Kwan, LinkedIn profile, https://www.linkedin.com/in/sara-kwan-mba-45a1736/

155   Kathy Knapp, LinkedIn profile, https://www.linkedin.com/in/kathy-knapp-029b5a25/

156   "Reese Witherspoon, *Glamour* Women of the Year, 2015," Facebook video, accessed September 13, 2019, https://www.facebook.com/watch/?v=10155637551490479.

157   Peter M. Senge et al., *The Fifth Discipline Fieldbook: Strategies for Building a Learning Organization* (New York: Doubleday, 1994).

158   Kimberly Faith, "Hay House Inspirational Testimonial Video for SWP Conference 2016," YouTube video, September 10, 2016, https://www.youtube.com/watch?v=bJka9GI39iE&feature=youtu.be.

Additional resources to assist on your journey.
Your soul will know which one is right for you.
Trust what you Know . . .

- *WhitneyLamb.com*
- *SkyFarmCare.com*
- *YourCosmicCafe.com*
- *BeckyStrauss.love*
- *IeamKelli.com*
- *TaraLRobinson.com*
- *ConsciousInk.com*

For your professional journey:

- *Upstreamhr.com/bold-career-journey*
- *BreakthruBranding.com/career*

Coupon code **CORPORATE**
for 50% discount

*For one-on-one executive
coaching, email:*

Kim@KimberlyFaith.com